YESTERDAY & TODAY

THE AUTO EDITORS OF CONSUMER GUIDE®
FOREWORD BY DARRELL WALTRIP

Publications International, Ltd.

The editors gratefully acknowledge the cooperation of the following photographers and photo sources that helped make this book possible:

Auto Club Speedway, Dale Barbee, Tyler Barrick/Autostock, Gary Beem, Jack Cansler, Phil Cavali, Chrysler Photographic, Chrysler-Plymouth Performance Publicity, Daytona Beach News Journal, Dodge Public Relations, Chris Dolack, ESPN, Greg Fielden, Ford Motor Company, LaDon George, Chris Graythen/Getty Images, David Griffin, Matt Griffith, Phil Hall, Bryan Hallman, Mark Hawkins, Gil Haywood, Christopher Hiltz, HHP Images/Harold Hinson, Mike Horne, IMS Photo, International Speedway Corporation, Rusty Jarrett/Getty Images for NASCAR, Dave Jensen, Brett Kelley, Don Kelly, Kentucky Speedway, Tom Kirkland, Mike Laczynski, Las Vegas Motor Speedway, Streeter Lecka/Getty Images, Vince Manocchi, Larry McTighe, Motorsports Images & Archives Photography, NASCAR, Bill Niven, Don Parnall/Costello Photo, Petty Enterprises, James Price, David Schenk, Texas Motor Speedway, Kevin Thorne, George Tiedemann/Sports Illustrated, Chris Trotman/Getty Images for NASCAR, Wieck Media Services, Inc., Doug Yockey.

Thanks to Marty Novak and Don Sikora II for making available their NASCAR memorabilia.

Special thanks to Bryan Hallman for his extensive knowledge of all that is NASCAR and his patient willingness to share it.

Louis Weber, CEO
Publications International, Ltd.
8140 Lehigh Avenue
Morton Grove, Illinois 60053

Contents

Foreword 6

THE DRIVERS 8

Red Byron 10

Marshall Teague 11

Fonty Flock 12

Tim Flock. 13

Herb Thomas 14

Lee Petty 15

Buck Baker. 16

Fireball Roberts 17

Joe Weatherly. 18

Ned Jarrett. 19

Junior Johnson 20

Rex White 21

Fred Lorenzen 22

Cale Yarborough 23

Richard Petty 24

LeeRoy Yarbrough 25

David Pearson 26

Bobby Isaac 27

Bobby Allison. 28

Benny Parsons 29

Darrell Waltrip 30

Dale Earnhardt. 31

Bill Elliott. 32

Terry Labonte 33

Rusty Wallace 34

Mark Martin. 35

Dale Jarrett 36

Alan Kulwicki 37

Jeff Gordon 38

Dale Earnhardt, Jr. 39

Tony Stewart 40

Jimmie Johnson 41

THE CARS 42

1948. 44

1949-1951 45

1952-1954 46

1955-1956 47

1957-1958 48

1959-1960 49

1961-1962 50

1963-1965 51

1966. 52

1967. 53

1968. 54

1969. 55

1970. 56

1971. 57

1972. 58

1973-1974 59

1975-1976 60

1977-1978 61

1979-1980 62

1981-1982 63

1983-1985 64

1986-1987 65

1988-1989 66

1990-1992 67

1993-1996 68

1997-1999 69

2000-2002 70

2003-2006 71

2007. 72

2008-2009 73

2010-2012 74

2013— 75

THE TRACKS 76

Daytona Beach & Road Course . . .78

North Wilkesboro Speedway . . 79

Lakewood Speedway 80

Raleigh Speedway 81

Martinsville Speedway 82

Langhorne Speedway 83

Darlington Raceway 84

Richmond International
    Raceway 85

Watkins Glen International . . . 86

Daytona International
    Speedway 87

Atlanta Motor Speedway 88

Charlotte Motor Speedway . . . 89

Bristol Motor Speedway 90

North Carolina Speedway 91

Dover International Speedway . . 92

Michigan International
    Speedway 93

Talladega Superspeedway 94

Pocono Raceway 95

Phoenix International
    Raceway 96

Sonoma Raceway 97

New Hampshire Motor
    Speedway 98

Indianapolis Motor
    Speedway 99

Texas Motor Speedway 100

Auto Club Speedway 101

Las Vegas Motor
    Speedway 102

Homestead-Miami
    Speedway 103

Chicagoland Speedway 104

Kansas Speedway 105

Kentucky Speedway 106

MEMORABILIA 107

THE EVENTS 110

Before NASCAR 112

1947 113

1948 114

1949 115

1950 116

1951 117

1952-1954 118

1955-1957 119

1958-1959 120

1960-1964 121

1965-1968 122

1969 123

1970-1971 124

1972 125

1973-1974 126

1975-1976 127

1977-1979 128

1980-1982 129

1983-1984 130

1985 131

1986-1987 132

1988-1989 133

1990-1993 134

1994-1997 135

1998-1999 136

2000-2001 137

2002-2003 138

2004-2005 139

2006-2007 140

2008-2009 141

2010-2012 142

2013 143

2014 144

Foreword

The year was 1972, and I was about to take the green flag at Talladega Superspeedway for my first-ever race in NASCAR's premier series. Buddy, ol' DW was in the big time now.

I was in a car I'd bought from Holman-Moody for $12,500. This baby was race-ready, came with a spare motor and a rich pedigree. The chassis had won the 1967 Daytona 500 with Mario Andretti behind the wheel. It had a Ford Fairlane body on it then, but Holman-Moody had bought it and turned it into a Mercury Cyclone. David Pearson, the Silver Fox, had even driven the car. Now, folks who know me know that Pearson was my hero, so that made the car even more magical.

Back in the day, Holman-Moody was a top-flight team. Today you would compare them to Hendrick Motorsports, Roush Fenway Racing, or Joe Gibbs Racing. So I knew that any car from them was going to be a good one. Even though $12,500 seemed like pile of money to me, I still considered it a bargain.

We had painted "Terminal Transport" on the car as the sponsor. They were a subsidiary of Texas Gas that my father-in-law ran. Terminal Transport was based in Atlanta, and the folks at Texas Gas had figured they would benefit the most from the sponsorship.

Back then, I had this old Maxwell House coffee truck. It was a two-ton truck with a big box body on the back, which, as you can imagine, was perfect for carrying all my race equipment plus towing a race car. I tried to paint over the logos, but trust me, you could still see "Maxwell House" underneath.

Well, I had borrowed a trailer from P. B. Crowell, who I had driven for, so with my wife Stevie by my side and our dog Charlie Brown, we left Nashville and headed south to Talladega. You want to talk old school? Let me tell you, *that* was old school.

Close your eyes for a second and picture me behind the wheel, Stevie and Charlie Brown next to me. I am driving an old Maxwell House coffee truck towing a 1971 Mercury Cyclone that used to be a Ford Fairlane. What a sight we must have been pulling into the garage area. Today these huge transporters go up and down the highway with their sponsor logos all over them. Funny thing though, I never got a cent from Maxwell House.

So here I am coming to take the first of 809 green flags in NASCAR's premier series. But then, in the blink of an eye, it was over. Twenty-nine years had passed. Where did they all go? Nevertheless, with the help of so many people, I was able to reach the pinnacle in my profession.

What literally started with talking my Dad into buying a go-kart we definitely couldn't afford had turned into three championships and 84 career wins in NASCAR's premier series. But see, the thing was, racing just came natural to me; it was just something I could do and do well. I raced a little bit on dirt but really didn't like it. I always told everyone that I never liked getting my uniform all dirty. But put me on asphalt, and I was a natural.

Golly…it seemed like just yesterday that we went from bringing that go-kart home, to unloading my Mercury in Talladega, to walking through the garage area in November 2000 saying goodbye to everyone after my final race.

Poor, poor pitiful me, huh? Well, sometimes in the rush of the here and now, you forget to raise your head up and look at your full body of work. When I do that, I am the first one to say that I have been blessed. I have been blessed by the Lord, blessed with my family, and blessed in my professional career.

And now I have been blessed with a second career: that of a TV broadcaster as part of the NASCAR on FOX team. Now, instead of focusing on just my car, I get to focus on all 43 cars. I will be the first to admit, I was pretty scared when I decided to retire. Racing was all I knew. Well, to be fair, racing and talking. So what a perfect marriage, huh? Me and a microphone.

I love NASCAR. I am very passionate about our sport. We have the greatest fans of any major sport. Now, sure, the folks in Daytona Beach and I occasionally butt heads; we always have and probably always will. But our sport has come a long way in 65 years.

Look at the positive impact from something as simple as implementing the double-file restarts for 2009. Everyone says it was probably the best

thing NASCAR has done in ages, but it about took an act of Congress to make it happen. And go back to February of the same year. When NASCAR eliminated testing and took the teams off the road, everyone couldn't wait to get to Daytona for Speedweeks. They were pumped up and excited to get there and get going. They weren't already burned out from testing so much.

Oh, by the way (and with ol' DW, there is always an "Oh, by the way"), remember my old Mercury and its rich history? Well, believe it or not, its history continues. I had wrecked it at Daytona, and afterward it sat outside Robert Gee's garage. For those of you who don't know, Robert Gee was Dale Earnhardt, Jr.'s, grandfather. Well, in 1989, Hurricane Hugo came through the Charlotte area and put a tree through the old girl.

Imagine my utter disbelief when Robert called me and said he was taking that car to the junkyard. I don't think so, Robert! Today, that baby is one of my most prized possessions in my museum in Harrisburg, North Carolina. Without question, it was worth every penny getting her restored.

And just like that car, there is a rich history in NASCAR, both yesterday and today.

Darrell Waltrip

CHAPTER ONE

THE DRIVERS

In the early years of stock car racing, many champion drivers learned their craft and honed their skills practicing on dusty back roads. As the sport became more popular during the 1950s, drivers tended to get their start on local dirt tracks before landing a NASCAR ride.

Today, many of the stars began running go-karts at an early age, then worked their way up the racing ladder before entering NASCAR Sprint Cup Series competition. But regardless of their background, the drivers featured in this section all exhibited the skill to pilot a car at breakneck speeds and the courage to live their lives at the ragged edge.

Red Byron was NASCAR's first champion, earning the title in the inaugural 1948 season and in '49. With most races of the day being run on dusty dirt tracks, drivers often exited their cars after the event looking as though they'd spent the day in a coal mine.

Red Byron

Due to injuries sustained during World War II, Red Byron often drove with his left leg in a brace that was then bolted to the clutch pedal. Byron was a master on dirt tracks and won the driver's championship in NASCAR's first two seasons.

Robert N. Byron's name is prominently etched in NASCAR's record books. Byron won the inaugural championship in 1948 and the first NASCAR Strictly Stock title (now known as the NASCAR Sprint Cup Series) in '49. Going by the nickname "Red" throughout his life, he refined the art of slinging dirt.

Byron, from Anniston, Alabama, claimed he first drove an automobile at age five and owned a car when he was 10. His professional racing career began when he was only 16. In the 1930s, he was interested in any form of speed on four wheels, be it open wheelers, chopped-up roadsters, powerful Midgets, or stock cars. During his early adulthood, Byron rose through the ranks of educational (small-time) racing and developed into a consistent winner.

With the outbreak of World War II, Byron enlisted in the U.S. Army Air Forces and served as a flight engineer on a B-24 bomber. He completed 57 missions in Europe but was shot down on his 58th over the Aleutian Islands. Critically wounded, Byron spent more than two years in army hospitals.

He left the hospital in 1945, able to walk on his own with the aid of a cane. Byron had exhibited countless feats of courage and resilience in the war, and he laid plans to return to auto racing.

In February 1946, Byron made a triumphant return to racing in a Modified event in Orlando, Florida. He nosed out Roy Hall and Bill France in a three-car finish. When he parked in the make-do confines of a roped-off Victory Lane, Byron had to be helped from his car. His left leg, badly damaged in the war, had been placed in a steel stirrup that was bolted to the clutch pedal. When he unbuckled the chin strap of his Cromwell helmet, he looked like a man twice his age of 30.

Despite his game leg and frail appearance, Red Byron could dazzle and bewilder the best stock jockeys in the business. He developed patience and savvy to complement his undiminished aggression, and it paid off with back-to-back NASCAR championships.

Byron competed in only 15 races from 1949 to '51 in NASCAR Strictly Stock and NASCAR Sprint Cup Series competition. He posted two wins and registered nine top-10 finishes.

Declining health forced him to hang up his goggles in 1951, but he remained active in racing. When he died of a heart attack in a Chicago hotel room on November 7, 1960, at the age of 44, he was managing a team in Sports Car Club of America competition.

Byron won NASCAR's inaugural Strictly Stock championship driving the #22 Oldsmobile.

Marshall Teague

Marshall Teague never won a NASCAR championship, but he did win an impressive seven of the 23 races he entered. Teague was a gifted mechanic and one of the first drivers to tap the potential of Hudson's revolutionary Hornet.

Marshall Pleasant Teague, one of racing's most brilliant minds, was also one of NASCAR's most accomplished race car drivers. A native of Daytona Beach, Teague began his racing career on December 2, 1945, at Seminole Speedway in Orlando, Florida. Still a Second Lieutenant in the United States Army, Teague was one of 22 drivers entered in the Orlando event. His name appeared on the entry list as "Lt. Marshall Teague," joining headliners Bill France, Roy Hall, Fonty Flock, Sgt. Red Byron, and Buddy Shuman. Teague finished second to France in his first effort.

The mechanically inclined Teague was a semi-regular competitor in stock car racing events in the late 1940s, winning races from 1946 to '48 with regularity. By the time the newfangled late-model NASCAR Strictly Stock division became the hot tour in '49 and '50, Teague had prepared a low-profile Hudson Hornet to drive in Bill France's organization.

Teague won his fifth career start at Daytona, driving the Hornet to a decisive victory. During the 1951 NASCAR campaign, Teague won five of his 15 starts and provided technical assistance and a car for Herb Thomas to drive in selected '51 races during Thomas's title run. Teague didn't show up in the final points standings since he elected to go against France's orders to refrain from driving in Mexico's Carrera Panamericana in the

winter of '51. The Mexican race was an exercise NASCAR approved of in 1950, but the '51 contest was strictly "hands off." Teague competed anyway and finished sixth in his class. The Mexican road-race incident strained the relationship between Teague and France, a rift that would last until the day Teague died in 1959.

Teague had to pay a hefty fine of nearly $600 to be reinstated by NASCAR for the 1952 Daytona Beach race. Teague successfully defended his Daytona championship, then won at Jacksonville and was among the contenders for the NASCAR championship.

All that changed on April 12, 1952. NASCAR's Bill Tuthill mailed a letter to Teague informing him that his championship points had been taken away due to participation in a non-NASCAR-sanctioned race at Tampa, a charge Teague denied.

In reaction to the letter, Teague quit NASCAR, joined the AAA Stock Car tour, and blazed a path of success in stock and open-wheel cars.

It was Teague's "Fabulous Hudson Hornet" that inspired the character of Doc Hudson in the 2006 animated film, Cars.

Fonty Flock

A cornerstone of the folklore of NASCAR's early years, Truman Fontello Flock was more than an accomplished throttle stomper. Known as Fonty, he was intelligent, well-spoken, and one of the few drivers of the late 1940s who felt at ease with the media. Always humorous and witty, he conducted himself admirably and helped NASCAR become a marketable commodity in its formative days.

Fonty was the second of three Flock brothers—and one sister—who tore up the dirt tracks in the early years of stock car racing. While he never won a NASCAR championship, he did win championships in other racing series.

As a teenager, Fonty sharpened his natural talents on rough dirt tracks under the tutelage of his older brother Bob. By the time he was 20, in 1941, Flock was regarded as one of stock car racing's best drivers. His rapid ascent to elite status took him to Bill France's touring series.

Fonty was crowned the champion of the 1947 National Championship Stock Car Circuit, the forerunner to NASCAR. He finished second in the '48 NASCAR standings and won the '49 Modified title. During the first three years in which France conducted Modified races, Flock won 34 races in just over 100 starts.

When the new Strictly Stock Late Model tour became part of NASCAR's traveling show in 1949, Flock was again one of the central figures, finishing fifth in the inaugural Strictly Stock standings. Flock scored his first NASCAR win in 1950 at Langhorne Speedway, then enjoyed his finest season in '51. Winning eight races and 13 poles, Flock took a close second to Herb Thomas in the '51 title chase.

Flock was leading the points standings and on pace to capture the 1952 NASCAR championship when he was injured in a crash at Martinsville. He missed one race and only drove for half of another but still ended the season fourth in the NASCAR standings.

Fonty quit NASCAR early in the 1954 season and campaigned in a Midwestern stock car series. He returned to NASCAR in '55 and won three races. After the '55 season, Flock only competed in select events. He won one of seven starts in '56 and remained inactive for most of the '57 season.

With the eighth annual Southern 500 coming up on Labor Day 1957, Herb Thomas asked Flock to drive his Pontiac in the race. Having won the event in '52, Flock jumped at the chance, but Darlington's fickle blacktop held a trump card.

On the 28th lap, Flock spun his car at the entrance to turn three and was struck hard by two other cars. He was taken for medical treatment and announced his retirement from a hospital bed.

Tim Flock

Tim Flock was the youngest—and ultimately most successful—of the famous Flock brothers. He won the NASCAR championship in 1952 and 1955, and was inducted posthumously into the NASCAR Hall of Fame in 2014.

Veteran NASCAR drivers will often talk of the "school of hard knocks"—a new driver's initiation into racing. Experienced drivers aren't afraid to swap sheet metal with rookies.

But perhaps no other driver was subjected to the kind of on-track training that Julius Timothy Flock was given. Tim Flock was the youngest of the Flock clan, the most famous family in the early days of stock car racing. Older brothers Bob and Fonty, plus sister Ethel Flock Mobley, all drove in NASCAR competition.

"I worshiped Bob and Fonty when they were driving," recalled Tim. "But they said I'd never be a race driver. I always tried extra hard to beat Fonty on the track because he wouldn't let me race as a kid."

Despite the objections of his siblings, the youngest Flock was determined to squeeze his way into the sport of speed. Finally convinced Tim was going to become a race car driver, Bob and Fonty decided it would be best to tutor their younger brother in the art of race track survival. "They took me out to the old Lakewood track in Atlanta and showed me all the tricks," remarked Tim. "I learned quite a bit in a short period of time."

Flock learned enough, apparently, to win the 1952 NASCAR championship. He was a contender again in '53, until an off-track incident laid him up for several weeks. When he came back in 1954, Flock finished first in the NASCAR race at Daytona's Beach & Road course but was disqualified when NASCAR officials determined his carburetor wasn't stock. Flock quit racing in disgust.

But in 1955, Flock returned to NASCAR to drive Chryslers for Carl Kiekhaefer. Flock enjoyed a phenomenal year, winning 18 races and 18 poles, both records at the time. He easily captured his second NASCAR championship.

In early 1956, Flock bailed out of the Kiekhaefer team, citing health reasons. He was only a part-time participant in NASCAR for the remainder of his career. His final victory came later in 1956 on the road course in Elkhart Lake, Wisconsin, beating the Kiekhaefer team in their own backyard. In 1961, Flock was booted out of NASCAR by Bill France for assisting Curtis Turner in his efforts to organize the drivers to join the Teamsters Union. When the ban was lifted in '65, Flock decided not to return to racing.

During his career, Flock won 39 races in 187 starts, giving him an impressive 20.745 winning percentage—second only to Herb Thomas on the all-time list. He remains one of stock car racing's most honored legends.

> "I couldn't take Kiekhaefer's drill-sergeant attitude anymore. I had to quit to save my own life"

Tim Flock won his first of two championships at the wheel of the #91 Hudson Hornet.

Herb Thomas

During his on-again, off-again racing career, Herb Thomas won two championships and registered the highest winning percentage of any driver in NASCAR history. Thomas was inducted posthumously into the NASCAR Hall of Fame in 2013.

Herb Thomas, of Olivia, North Carolina, was the hardest charger in NASCAR's early days and quickly became its first superstar. When he didn't win, he usually either blew up the car or wrecked. "It's win or bust with me," Thomas said. "Second place is never good enough."

Thomas began racing Modifieds after World War II with limited success. When Bill France orchestrated the Strictly Stock circuit in 1949, Thomas built a late-model automobile for competition. He struggled once again, coming up winless until late in the 1950 season when he won at Martinsville.

The Martinsville triumph set the stage for the 1951 season. Thomas drove three different brands of cars—Hudson, Plymouth, and Oldsmobile—and put them all into Victory Lane. He won seven events in 33 starts and snared the 1951 NASCAR championship. He won the championship again in '53 and was runner-up in '52 and '54, amassing 32 more wins in the process. Still in his early 30s, Thomas was looking toward a bright racing future—until fate intervened.

Early in the 1955 season, Thomas had a bad spill at Charlotte's dirt track. From his hospital bed, he made a bold prediction: "Don't worry about me, I'll be racing again by the time the Darlington 500 comes up in September. And I'll win it again, too."

Both predictions came true. And despite missing 22 of the 45 races in 1955, Thomas still finished fifth in the final points standings.

Thomas's last full year in racing was 1956, a season in which he should have won the title a third time. Instead, another accident ended the career of one of America's best stock car drivers.

Thomas started the 1956 campaign in his own Chevrolets but joined Carl Kiekhaefer's powerful Chrysler and Dodge team at midseason. After winning three races for Kiekhaefer, Thomas tired of the owner's dictatorial attitude and returned to his self-owned team. With five races left, Thomas was on top of the points standings when he entered a 100-miler at the Cleveland County Fairgrounds. Thomas was running second when his car was bumped from behind, sending it through the guardrail and into the path of oncoming racers. His resulting injuries caused him to miss the rest of the season, but he still ended up second in the final points standings.

Though Thomas recovered, he had lost his edge. After running two races in 1957, he retired. He came back to run one race in '62, then quit for good.

In all, Herb Thomas won 48 NASCAR races in 228 career starts. His 21.053 winning percentage remains the best on the all-time list.

During the 1951 season, Thomas drove the #92 Hudson Hornet— along with a Plymouth and Oldsmobile—to his first NASCAR championship.

Lee Petty

Although he won the inaugural Daytona 500 and three NASCAR championships, Lee Petty claimed he was most proud of the racing empire he founded. He was likely also proud of his son, Richard Petty, who went on to become stock car racing's most successful driver. In 2011, Lee Petty was inducted posthumously into the NASCAR Hall of Fame, a year after his son Richard became one of the inaugural inductees.

In NASCAR's wild and woolly early days, many of the competitors were hardcore critters who wouldn't think twice about slamming another driver off the track. Lee Petty was different. As a refreshing, out-of-the-ordinary member of NASCAR's wild bunch, he was never regarded as one of stock car racing's hardest chargers. Instead, he was considered a great calculator who applied the strategies of a chess player. "I have to finish in the top three cars to make money," Petty said in a 1954 interview. "I have to finish among the first five to break even. After that, I'm going in the red."

Petty drove to finish—and to finish well. During the heavy factory participation in the '50s, Petty's independent team lacked the pure speed of the industry-supported outfits, yet he still racked up more than his share of victories—enough to earn him the NASCAR championship in 1954, '58, and '59. At the time of his retirement in 1964, he was NASCAR's most prolific race winner with 54 victories to his credit, and he finished in the top 10 an incredible 332 times in 427 starts.

"Papa" Petty began his racing career at the ripe age of 33. He participated in the inaugural NASCAR Strictly Stock event on June 19, 1949, driving a huge Buick Roadmaster Petty claimed "me and some buddies had gone in on together." During the race, Petty lost control and flipped. In one of racing's grand quotes, Petty recalled his feelings at that moment: "I was just sitting there thinking about having to go back home and explain to my wife where I'd been with the car."

But Petty's racing luck quickly improved. He scored his first career win later that year in Heidelberg, Pennsylvania, and registered at least one win each year in his first 13 seasons of NASCAR stock car competition.

Petty was one of the few pioneer drivers who was able to successfully continue his career into the progressive 1960s, making the bumpy transition from the dusty bullrings to the lightning-fast superspeedways. When the Daytona International Speedway opened in '59, Petty drove an Oldsmobile to a two-foot victory over Johnny Beauchamp. But two years later, he was involved in an accident that temporarily sidelined the veteran driver. Afterward, Petty strapped on his goggles for six more races. "I drove again just to prove I wasn't scared," he quipped.

"We were not like some of the others," Petty said several years after his retirement. "Some of the other boys, they drove and took everything out of racing they could. They spent their money for pleasure. We spent ours to build. Everything we've done has been aimed at racing. We started under an ol' reaper shed with no floor in it and we built it up. That was probably what I was most proud of." Indeed, Petty's racing empire would go on to help support a number of stock car drivers, including his son, Richard, and grandson, Kyle.

Above: *Lee Petty primarily drove Plymouths, Chryslers, and Oldsmobiles during his career, but they all carried his signature #42 on the door.* **Bottom:** *Petty piloted an Oldsmobile to victory in the first Daytona 500 in 1959.*

Buck Baker

Above: *Buck Baker was known for both his on-track skills and his off-track confrontations. His son Buddy, who also became a renowned driver, once said, "My dad won his share of races on the track, but I don't think he ever lost a battle in the pits."* **Below right:** *Baker won the 1956 NASCAR championship while driving Chryslers for the famed Kiekhaefer team.*

Elzie Wylie Baker, better known as "Buck" in NASCAR racing circles, was one of the toughest and most capable high-speed chauffeurs of the 1950s. A hard-nosed competitor in the rough-and-tumble Modified division, Baker won his share of battles both on the race track and in postrace fisticuffs.

During the progressive 1950s, Baker was active in all branches of the NASCAR racing tree. He divided his time between the tumultuous short tracks and the popular NASCAR stock car circuit—and also took time out to win the championship for NASCAR's short-lived open-wheel Speedway Division tour in '52. A driver held in high esteem among team owners, Baker became a sought-after pilot when he wasn't campaigning his own machinery.

In 1955, Carl Kiekhaefer joined the NASCAR touring series and virtually cleaned house. Kiekhaefer's team won 22 of the 39 races, leaving only scraps for the other shade-tree-engineered teams. Kiekhaefer noticed, however, that Baker was giving the Kiekhaefer outfit a good run for the money in his self-owned Oldsmobiles and Buicks. "I saw that Buck was my top competition," Kiekhaefer said at the beginning of the '56 NASCAR season. "There is only one thing to do with a man like that—hire him!"

Baker won his first start with Kiekhaefer in a 150-miler at Phoenix's dirt track. It set the stage for the remainder of the campaign as Baker won 14 races and captured the 1956 NASCAR title. He finished in the top five in 31 of his 48 starts.

Kiekhaefer suddenly quit NASCAR after the 1956 season, and Baker found himself in a factory-supported Chevrolet. Baker continued his hot streak, though, winning 10 races and racking up his second straight championship.

In addition to his two championships, Baker won the storied Southern 500 at Darlington three times: in 1953, 1960, and 1964. The last proved to be the final victory of his career, which spanned 636 NASCAR races and included a total of 46 wins.

Baker retired as a full-time driver from NASCAR competition after the 1968 season. He continued to race, however, first in the pony league Grand Touring series (which featured Mustangs and Camaros) and later on short tracks in the Carolinas. In 1976, he made a surprise NASCAR comeback, entering the Dixie 500 at Darlington Raceway in South Carolina. After qualifying 13th, Baker went on to finish sixth—not bad for a battle-weary 57-year-old veteran.

Buck Baker entered his first NASCAR race in 1949 and ran his last in 1976—at 57 years young. He was inducted into the NASCAR Hall of Fame posthumously in 2013.

Fireball Roberts

A blazing fastball as a baseball pitcher earned Fireball Roberts his nickname, but he was equally speedy on the track. Roberts was posthumously inducted into the NASCAR Hall of Fame in 2014.

The inscription on Fireball Roberts's tombstone says it all: "He brought stock car racing a freshness, distinction, a championship quality that surpassed the rewards collected by the checkered flag."

Edward Glenn Roberts was one of NASCAR's most electrifying speed merchants in the 1950s and early '60s. As stock car racing began squeezing its way into the sports mainstream, Roberts was the most recognized name in the rough-and-tumble sport.

Roberts's "Fireball" nickname originated during his years as a baseball pitcher, when he was known for his blazing fastball. He applied the same kamikaze attitude whether on the mound or racing stock cars—he was wild, rambunctious, and electrifying.

Roberts began racing in 1947 while still in his teens, gaining notoriety for his blend of bravery, lightning-quick reflexes, and precise judgment. He advanced to NASCAR in 1950 at the tender age of 21, scoring his first win that same year in only his third career start. When the factory Ford team added him to its roster in 1956, he responded with 13 wins over the next two seasons. Roberts signed with Frank Strickland's Chevrolet team in '58, winning six of his 10 starts.

In 1959, Fireball teamed with Pontiac and the famed mechanic Smokey Yunick. A shining example of excellence, Roberts and Yunick set dozens of speed records. Roberts won nine poles and three races in 17 starts during '59 and '60.

Despite being one of NASCAR's epic risk takers, Roberts was a thinking man's driver. He was also a master on the high-speed Daytona International Speedway, winning several races there, including the 1962 Daytona 500.

Roberts joined the Ford team in 1963 and won four races in 20 starts. As a member of the Holman-Moody team, Roberts and teammate Fred Lorenzen ruled the NASCAR roost.

Roberts was mulling the prospect of retirement in 1964 when he entered the World 600. He wanted one last crack at Charlotte Motor Speedway, the only superspeedway in the South where he had failed to score a win. Early in the race, Roberts swerved to dodge two spinning cars. He avoided a direct hit but careened into the edge of a concrete wall inside the backstretch and passed away several weeks later. NASCAR had lost one of its top drivers at the all-too-early age of 35.

Fireball Roberts was a master of the high-speed ovals. In 1962, he drove a Smokey Yunick-prepared Pontiac at Daytona, where he won three preliminary races and the Daytona 500.

Joe Weatherly

Joe Weatherly began his racing career on motorcycles but, after graduating to NASCAR, won championships in the only two seasons he raced the full schedule.

Of the men who have won the NASCAR championship, few if any were more determined than Joe Herbert Weatherly. The stubby Norfolk, Virginia, leadfoot succeeded in anything he tried, on two wheels or four.

Weatherly's indoctrination into the sport of speed came in motorcycle racing. After winning the American Motorcycle Association championship twice, he looked to stock cars for his livelihood.

In the early '50s, Weatherly earned his living racing Modifieds (he won the NASCAR Modified championship in 1953) but also dabbled a little in NASCAR stock car competition. His first NASCAR stock car start was in the '52 Southern 500, where he finished 16th. From that auspicious beginning, Weatherly soon became known as one of the craftiest drivers on the circuit.

After a stint in NASCAR's Convertible division, Weatherly made the full-time move to the headlining NASCAR circuit. In 1961, Weatherly hooked up with team owner Bud Moore and despite entering just 25 races—out of a total of 52—managed to win nine times, good enough for an amazing fourth in the final points standings. In '62, the team ran a full schedule, and again Weatherly won nine races, along with enough points to walk away with the championship in his first full-season attempt.

When General Motors sliced its racing budget in 1963, Moore was forced to cut back his schedule and forsake the 100-milers on short tracks to concentrate on the big-money superspeedway events. Without a ride for the short tracks, the gritty Weatherly improvised. He "hitchhiked" his way into 18 races, driving equipment that wasn't cham-

pionship caliber. During the course of the season, Weatherly drove for nine different teams, piloting five different makes of cars. For his efforts, he won the championship for the second year in a row.

Weatherly took the role of a modest champion. "I was lucky to get rides when I needed them. Lots of guys in racing helped me. I don't know how to thank each and every one for their help. I tried to split up the money so they would all be satisfied."

Weatherly started the 1964 NASCAR campaign with consistent finishes and was once again leading the standings when he died as a result of injuries from an accident.

During his tragedy-shortened NASCAR career, Weatherly won 25 races in 229 starts. He was inducted into the NASCAR Hall of Fame in 2015.

The Bud Moore pit crew services Joe Weatherly's Pontiac in 1962, the year he won nine races and his first NASCAR championship.

Ned Jarrett

Ned Jarrett won two NASCAR champion-ships in the 1960s, and his son Dale would add to the family legacy in the '90s. Ned Jarrett was inducted into the NASCAR Hall of Fame in 2011, with Dale fol-lowing him three years later.

After winning the NASCAR Sportsman championships in 1957 and '58, Ned Jarrett looked for more lucrative horizons in the world of stock car racing.

A farm boy out of Newton, North Carolina, Jarrett was unable to convince a front-running car owner to give him a chance. So, with little money, he was forced to improvise. "Paul Spaulding, who owned a Ford that Junior Johnson drove for a year or so, decided he was going to build a new Dodge for late 1959," Jarrett explained. "He had his Ford up for sale with a $2000 price tag.

"I wanted that Ford in the worst way," Jarrett continued. "Only problem was, I didn't have $2000." But he did have a plan.

The first weekend of August 1959, a pair of NASCAR events were slated on successive nights in Myrtle Beach and Charlotte. Each 100-miler paid $800 to win and as NASCAR Sportsman champion, Jarrett was eligible for a $100 appear-ance fee. "I quickly figured how I could work this thing out," said Jarrett. "I could give Mr. Spauld-ing a check for the car on Friday after the banks closed, post-date it for the following Monday, and go out and win both of those races. I would have $1800 and I could somehow come up with the other $200 to make the check good. It seemed so simple. I gave Mr. Spaulding a check for $2000 with no money in the bank to cover it."

Jarrett towed the car to Rambi Speedway in Myrtle Beach, started ninth, and, in Cinderella fashion, won the race. He pocketed the $900, but it was a costly victory. The tape used to wrap the steering wheel had sharp edges that cut

into his hands. "I was in no condition to drive at Charlotte," he recalled. "I could hardly grip the steering wheel with my hands bandaged up. But I had to have another $1100 in the bank Monday morning."

Jarrett started 10th in the Charlotte event, but his injured hands forced him out of the race early. Joe Weatherly, who was spectating from the pits, relieved Jarrett during the first caution. When Junior Johnson departed on lap 76 with a blown engine, he hopped into Jarrett's car for the balance of the race. "Junior brought the car home first," said Jarrett. "Joe was a little too short to reach the con-trols. I got paid the $900 and offered some to Junior for helping me out. He didn't accept any payment. And my check was good come Mon-day morning."

Jarrett went on to win 48 more NASCAR events and two champi-onships along the way. In 1961, he drove Bee Gee Holloway's Chevrolet to the championship and won the title again in '65 while driving a factory-backed Ford for Bondy Long.

Following the 1966 season, Jarrett unexpected-ly retired. "One thing I promised myself is that I would retire while I was at the top," he explained. "I didn't want to go out while on my way down."

Jarrett's second of two championships was won in 1965 while the driver suffered from a mid-season back injury. Weekly visits to the doctor allowed him to continue his quest for the title.

Junior Johnson

Although he never won a driver's championship, Junior Johnson was one of the most respected names in NASCAR, eventually winning six championships as a team owner. His dedication to the sport made him one of the inaugural inductees into the NASCAR Hall of Fame in 2010.

When writer Tom Wolfe dubbed Junior Johnson "The Last American Hero" in the March 1965 issue of *Esquire* magazine, the portly kid from Ronda, North Carolina, was already a legend.

Like many of the pioneers of stock car racing, Robert Glenn Johnson Jr. developed his driving skills on back-country dirt roads. He was one of many drivers who easily transferred his talents to the highly pitched pavement of the NASCAR superspeedways.

In his first full season, Johnson won five races and finished sixth in the 1955 NASCAR points standings. If NASCAR had awarded a Rookie of the Year trophy at the time, Johnson surely would have won it.

After an 11-month hiatus from racing, Johnson returned to the NASCAR scene in 1958 and picked up where he left off, winning six events. The following year he added five more. By this time, he was widely regarded as one of the most capable short-track race car drivers in the business.

Johnson was a master in the art of dirt-track racing, painting a perfect set of grooves in the tight corners of any dirt canvas. Fifteen of Johnson's first 16 NASCAR victories came on dirt tracks. As a result, he was often considered a one-dimensional driver—a prodigious craftsman on dirt, but not well-versed on superspeedways.

That all changed in the 1960 Daytona 500, when Johnson drove an outdated and underpowered Chevrolet to victory in the second running of NASCAR's biggest event. Follow-up wins at Charlotte and Darlington solidified the growing

notion that he could obviously mix more than a little brainpower with his brawn and win on pavement as well as dirt.

Johnson's finest season came in 1965 when he won 13 races. When he retired the following year at the age of 34, Johnson had accumulated 50 NASCAR victories, at that time the second best in NASCAR history. He often said, "I'd rather lead one lap and fall out of the race than stroke it and finish in the money." In 313 starts, Johnson finished among the top-three positions 91 times, but he failed to finish 165 events. "Go or blow was always my philosophy in racing," said Junior.

After Johnson hung up his goggles, he established his own racing team and became one of the most successful owners in NASCAR's Modern Era. Johnson's cars won six NASCAR championships, including a string with Cale Yarborough in 1976, '77, and '78, the first time a driver and owner won three consecutive titles.

Above: *Johnson's most successful season was in 1965, when he won 13 races in the #27 Holly Farms Poultry Ford.* **Below:** *Johnson scored one of his biggest victories in the 1960 Daytona 500. Here he hoists a soft drink in celebration.*

Rex White

Rex White stands as the shortest driver ever to win the NASCAR championship. Six wins and consistently high finishes earned him the 1960 crown.

Diminutive Rex White, the smallest man (5 feet, 4 inches tall and 135 pounds) to ever wear the NASCAR championship crown, looked more like comedian George Gobel than a race car driver. And by all rights, he shouldn't have been one. As a child, White was stricken with polio, but the little guy with the big heart didn't let the one-time crippling disease slow him down.

At the age of 25, White went racing for the first time in the NASCAR Sportsman Division, where he quickly became a force to be reckoned with. He went on to win the Sportsman championship in his rookie year.

Seemingly a natural on short tracks, White served a two-year apprenticeship on the small ovals near his home in Silver Spring, Maryland. In 1956, he came south, set up base in South Carolina, and began his personal quest to win the NASCAR title. Rex Allen White started 24 races in '56 and finished in the top 10 on 14 occasions—very impressive stats for a rookie in the big leagues of stock car racing. He also finished second in the final NASCAR Short Track standings, an offspring of the NASCAR Sprint Cup Series. He was runner-up again in 1959.

In the winter of '59, White, who ran his own operation, hired Louis Clements to be his chief mechanic and crew chief. "He's the best in the business," White said at the time. "I felt I needed a man like him to win the championship." Clements was offered an unusual deal. After expenses, White split all the profits 50/50 with Clements. White owned the car and drove it but paid Clements an amount equal to his own salary to keep it running.

The deal paid off. In 1960, White won six races and claimed the NASCAR championship. His earnings, after the points fund had been paid, came to a then-record $57,524.

Nineteen sixty-one and '62 were also good years for White, who won 15 times and finished second and fifth, respectively, in the points standings. In the '62 season finale at Atlanta Motor Speedway, White won the only superspeedway race of his career. Driving an underpowered Chevrolet in the days when Pontiac and Ford reigned supreme, White kept his car in the hunt all afternoon. With just three laps to go, he edged into the lead, holding off Joe Weatherly to snare the win.

White's lone big-track win was also the final win of his career. He raced only part time in 1963, finishing ninth in the final points standings. The following year, while driving a Mercury from the Bud Moore shops, White suddenly retired from NASCAR racing at the age of 35. The reason remains a mystery.

During his career, White won 28 NASCAR races in 233 starts. He was inducted into the NASCAR Hall of Fame in 2015.

White won the 1960 championship at the wheel of the #4 Chevrolet. Unlike many drivers who raced for factory-backed teams, White owned his own operation.

Fred Lorenzen

Compared to many top drivers of his day, "Fearless Freddy" Lorenzen had a rather brief and spotty NASCAR career but managed to score 26 wins in just 158 starts.

Fred Lorenzen began his erratic racing career on short tracks in Illinois, where he earned quite a reputation. This blossomed into a brief stab at the NASCAR circuit in 1956, but his money ran out after he had competed in just seven races.

Lorenzen went back home broken but undaunted. He graduated up stock car racing's ladder to win the USAC Stock Car championship crown in 1958 and '59. In 1960, Lorenzen moved south and took a job with the famous Holman-Moody Ford team as a mechanic. But he was restless in that role and quit, deciding instead to form his own team. Lorenzen made 10 NASCAR starts in 1960, after which he sold his car and headed back to his home town of Elmhurst, Illinois. He was out of racing, hungry, disgusted, and discouraged.

A few months later, Moody phoned Lorenzen and asked him if he was interested in becoming the lead driver on his team. "I was really surprised," said Lorenzen. "I couldn't imagine what I had done to impress them. I'm sure a lot of people thought they were crazy to hire me." Crazy like a fox, it turned out.

In only his second start with the Holman-Moody team, Lorenzen claimed his first career victory. He went on to win three of his 15 starts in '61, then two of 19 races in '62. Lorenzen hit his stride in 1963, winning six races in 29 starts

and finishing third in the final points standings, despite starting only about half the races.

Statistically, Lorenzen's most productive year was 1964, when he won eight of his 16 NASCAR starts. This included consecutive victories at Bristol, Atlanta, North Wilkesboro, Martinsville, and Darlington, a five-race tear that remains one of the most dominating performances in the history of NASCAR.

After winning the Daytona 500 in 1965 and compiling a career record of 26 victories in 158 starts, Lorenzen suddenly retired from competition. The racing bug brought him back to the circuit in 1970, but although he ran up front on a number of occasions, some of his competitive edge had been lost. In the fall of '72, Lorenzen bowed out for the final time.

Herb Nab, once Lorenzen's crew chief, had the highest regard for Fearless Freddy. "That's the best driver there is," Nab said. "He can drive a race car better than any of the others, including Fireball Roberts. Don't let anyone tell you different." Lorenzen was inducted into the NASCAR Hall of Fame in 2015.

Above: *Regardless of year, Fred Lorenzen could be found behind the wheel of the #28 Ford. In 1963, he finished third in the standings despite running only about half the season's races.* **Below left:** *Lorenzen only competed in 16 races in 1964 but won eight of them, an incredible feat.*

Cale Yarborough

Above: *Yarborough began his NASCAR career in 1957 while still in his teens, but it would be another 15 years before he hit his stride. Championships in 1976, '77, and '78 made him the first driver to score three in a row. He was inducted into the NASCAR Hall of Fame in 2012.*
Below right: *The #11 Chevrolet took Yarborough to his first championship in 1976.*

Born William Caleb Yarborough in Timmonsville, South Carolina, Yarborough made his NASCAR debut at the 1957 Southern 500 while still in his teens. He finished in 42nd place after a broken hub took him out of the race. Yarborough drove in only three more races over the next four years, never managing a top-10 finish. But that string was broken in 1962, when he placed tenth in a Daytona 500 qualifying race.

It wasn't until 1965 that Yarborough ran anything close to a full schedule, and he recorded his first win that year—along with one of the scarier moments of his career. While attempting to overtake the leader during the Southern 500, Yarborough's Ford glanced off the other car, sailed over the guardrail at Darlington Raceway, and came to rest against a telephone pole outside the track. "I knew I was in trouble when I saw grass, because I know there ain't no grass on a race track," said Yarborough, who escaped the incident uninjured. Though he didn't win any more races that year, Yarborough finished a respectable tenth in the points standings. After that, his race schedule was again cut back, but his win total kept climbing, reaching 14 by the end of 1970.

After starting just nine NASCAR races over the next two years (during which time he also competed in open-wheel Indy cars), Yarborough finally ran a full NASCAR schedule in 1973, and his career took off. He won four races that year, including the Southeastern 500, where he led every lap from green flag to checkered. He rose from virtual obscurity to a top contender almost overnight, finishing second in the points standings behind Richard Petty. During 1974's 30-race schedule, Yarborough racked up an amazing 10 victories, but again finished second to Petty in points.

After winning "only" three races in 1975, Yarborough charged back in '76, recording nine victories— and his first championship. He won the championship again in '77 and once more in '78, making him the first driver in NASCAR history to win three in a row. Though he would never get a fourth, Yarborough continued his winning ways, racking up 24 more victories before his retirement in 1988.

During more than three decades in NASCAR, Yarborough left his mark on the record books and became one of the most popular and best-known drivers on the circuit. He won the prestigious Daytona 500 four times and, in 1984, became the first to qualify for the race at more than 200 mph. A career total of 83 wins puts him sixth on the all-time list, and his 14 pole positions in 1980 remains a modern-era single-season record.

Above: *For nearly three decades, Yarborough stood alone as the only driver to win three NASCAR championships in a row. When his record was finally tied by Jimmie Johnson in 2008, Yarborough, who had been one of Johnson's childhood heroes, was on hand for the celebration.*

Richard Petty

Richard Petty brought himself and NASCAR stock car racing from the small two-paragraph stories at the back of the sports section to front-page headlines. His name, his smile, his mannerisms, and his driving record made every sports page reader south of Virginia take notice of the Southern brand of motorsports.

It took "King Richard" just 10 years to become the number-one driver in NASCAR history. His career began on July 12, 1958, 10 days after his 21st birthday. It was a NASCAR Convertible race at Columbia, South Carolina, and he finished sixth in an Oldsmobile. "I felt I was ready to race before that," remarked Petty. "But Daddy [Lee Petty] told me that I would have to wait until I was 21." Petty made only nine NASCAR stock car starts in 1958, then became the Sunoco Rookie of the Year in '59.

Petty's first NASCAR stock car race, oddly, was outside the continental United States. Six days after his baptism in Columbia, Petty drove

Above: *Richard Petty holds many NASCAR records that will probably never be broken. His name is synonomous with the #43 that graced the Plymouths he drove to his first championship in '64* **(right)** *and to his second in '67* **(below).**

the #142 Oldsmobile at the Canadian National Exposition track in Toronto. The fuzzy-cheeked youngster managed to go 55 laps before he "hit the fence." "It wasn't much of a race," Petty recalled. "I got in Daddy's way when he was lapping me, so he punted me into the fence. He went on to win, so I reckon it was a good day for the Pettys."

From that inauspicious beginning, Petty became the King of NASCAR racing, winning the championship in 1964, '67, '71, '72, '74, '75, and '79. Petty's achievements earned a write-up in *Newsweek* magazine, the first time the national weekly devoted an article to a stock car driver. He was also featured in *Sports Illustrated*, *Life* magazine, and *True Magazine for Men*.

"I know of no other driver in NASCAR history who has brought more recognition to the sport," said NASCAR founder Bill France in 1967.

Upon his retirement in 1992, Petty could look back over his 35-year racing career and count a record 200 wins in 1185 career starts, along with 712 top-10 finishes. Other highlights include a string of 10 consecutive victories on the way to 27 in total during the 1967 season, both records that "King Richard" will likely never see broken.

Above: *While he has hung up his helmet, Petty remains active in NASCAR, and was inducted into the NASCAR Hall of Fame in 2010.* **Below:** *Petty has raced a number of different makes. He won his seventh and final crown in '79 in a Chevrolet.*

LeeRoy Yarbrough

LeeRoy Yarbrough was tremendously successful in NASCAR's Modified division before he moved up to NASCAR Sprint Cup Series competition. His 14 career wins at the top level don't do his talents justice, as he was a skilled pilot who was once voted the best American driver.

Lonnie LeeRoy Yarbrough grew up on the rough side of Jacksonville, Florida, and developed an affinity for speed at an early age. When he was 12, Yarbrough put together his first car, a 1934 Ford with a Chrysler engine. As a teenager, he gave the local cops fits. At 19, Yarbrough found his way to a local dirt track to ventilate his lust for speed. Amazingly, Yarbrough won the very first race he ever ran at Jacksonville Speedway in the spring of 1957.

Yarbrough started his racing career in the lower tier NASCAR Sportsman Division. After winning 11 races, Yarbrough moved up to the more powerful Modifieds and won 83 features in a three-year span. He then advanced to NASCAR's top series.

A skillful driver, Yarbrough became an instant success. He won two short-track races in the 1964 NASCAR Sprint Cup Series season, the first year he competed in 34 races. Two years later, Yarbrough scored his first superspeedway win at Charlotte.

Yarbrough had a flair for the dramatic. In the 1969 Daytona 500, Yarbrough found himself trailing Charlie Glotzbach by 11 seconds with 10 laps remaining. He slashed his way through the slower traffic and drew in on the leader. On the final lap, Yarbrough ducked to the low side to make the decisive pass, but a lapped car loomed in his path. In an impressive display of skill, he dove to the low side in turn three to clear the lapped car, nearly clipping the apron. He took the lead from Glotzbach and dashed under the checkered flag a car length in front.

The passion he brought to the fight had elevated Yarbrough to the top echelon of his profession. He was the Daytona 500 champion, but he wasn't finished. Next, he won Darlington's Rebel 400, then Charlotte's World 600, lapping the entire field at least twice. He also bagged the summer 400-miler at Daytona.

Yarbrough won the summer race at Atlanta Motor Speedway despite a 102-degree fever. He captured the Southern 500 by passing David Pearson on the final lap. And he won by a full lap at Rockingham in October, overcoming a lap deficit when a flat tire sent him into the wall. By season's end, Yarbrough had seven wins to his credit.

> "I wanted to be a race car driver ever since I was 12. If you think enough about doing something, you should want to be the best."

LeeRoy Yarbrough truly made a name for himself with his outstanding 1969 performance. He won dozens of postseason awards and was voted the best American driver by a panel of experts.

After his sparkling 1969 season, Yarbrough's performance record tailed off. A victim of the factory withdrawal, Yarbrough had to scramble to locate rides. He won only once in '70, at Charlotte Motor Speedway, and only entered six races in '71. In 1972, he registered nine top-10 finishes in 18 starts.

Yarbrough showed up for Daytona's 1973 Speedweeks but failed to earn a starting berth for the Daytona 500. He virtually dropped out of sight after that, never again appearing at a NASCAR event.

Yarbrough won the 1969 Daytona 500 in the #98 Ford and went on to win six more races in what would be his best year in NASCAR's top series.

David Pearson

Above: *Despite competing only part-time for most of his NASCAR career, David Pearson won three championships, and his 105 victories puts him second on the all-time win list behind Richard Petty. The two champion drivers battled it out on numerous occasions, including at the 1973 Firecracker 400 at Daytona (below), in which Pearson in the #21 Mercury edged out Petty for the win. Pearson was inducted into the NASCAR Hall of Fame in 2011.*

David Pearson never had any inclination to drive on the NASCAR tour. But once his mind was changed, he became one of the top drivers in NASCAR history.

Pearson began his racing career in the 1950s and, unlike many drivers, had no aspirations beyond chasing prize money on the short-track NASCAR Sportsman circuit. "I used to listen to some of the big races on the radio," said Pearson. "I thought those guys must be crazy running 150 miles per hour at places like Daytona."

But Pearson's success in weekly short-track competitions gained him a large following of fans. And unbeknownst to him, this legion of supporters became his ticket to the big time.

In 1959, Pearson's fans began a fund-raising campaign to get Pearson in a NASCAR race car and collected nearly $1500. "I didn't want anything to do with that idea," said Pearson. "I wanted to give the money back to the people who donated it, but I didn't know where it all came from." With some additional funds pulled from the family bank account, Pearson bought a race-ready 1959 Chevrolet and made his plunge into NASCAR racing at Daytona's 1960 Speedweeks. He didn't set the world on fire but did perform admirably, well enough to earn him the 1960 Sunoco Rookie of the Year award.

Pearson went on to win three races in 1961, the last being the Dixie 400 at Atlanta Motor Speed-way. Pearson's victory at Atlanta was a noteworthy event: The speedy sophomore passed another driver on the final lap, making it the first time in superspeedway history that a race had been decided by a last-lap pass.

Pearson joined the Cotton Owens team in 1963, with which he won the '66 NASCAR championship. A year later, he replaced the retired Fred Lorenzen on the famed Holman-Moody team and won the championship in '68 and '69, becoming only the second driver in NASCAR history to win three titles.

Afterward, however, Pearson vowed never again to engage in the exhausting exercise of running the full tour. He had actively campaigned for the championship four times and had won three of them. In 1972, Pearson joined the Wood Brothers Mercury team, a partnership that became one of the most successful in history.

In 1973, Pearson enjoyed perhaps his finest year. While competing in selected events, Pearson won 10 of his 15 starts on superspeedways and 11 out of 18 for the year. His 61.1 percent remains the all-time record for winning percentage in a single season.

After recording his 100th win in 1978, Pearson quietly retired in 1986, having competed in 574 NASCAR races. All told, he won 105 times, which ranks second on the all-time list. It will forever remain a mystery how many races he could have won had he competed full time.

Pearson won his first NASCAR championship in 1966 in the #6 Dodge prepared by the Cotton Owens team.

Bobby Isaac

Bobby Isaac was a tough competitor who pulled himself up by his own bootstraps, rising from poverty to the top ranks of NASCAR competition.

Bobby Isaac's journey to becoming a NASCAR champion is a classic rags to riches story. The son of a mill worker and one of nine brothers and sisters, Isaac didn't own a pair of shoes until he was 13. Lacking parental supervision, he quit school in the sixth grade, racked balls in a pool hall, and did a lot of aimless hitchhiking.

It wasn't until 1956, at the age of 24, that Isaac began racing full time. He became a top driver during his tenure in the NASCAR Modified and NASCAR Sportsman bullrings. He also established new standards for being fined by NASCAR executive manager Pat Purcell. After a heated battle on the track, Isaac tended to settle "paybacks" with his fists. It took a few years for Purcell to break Isaac of this habit. "He told me that I needed racing a lot more than racing needed me," reflected Isaac.

In 1963, a more mature Isaac broke into the top ranks of NASCAR competition. His impressive finishes in equipment regarded as second rate caught the eye of Ray Nichels, who headed a Dodge and Plymouth factory team. Nichels seated Isaac in a Dodge for the '64 season.

Isaac won his very first start for Nichels in the 100-mile qualifying race at Daytona and went on to post five top-five finishes. In 1966, Isaac joined the Junior Johnson Ford team.

Meanwhile, Nord Krauskopf, owner of the K&K Insurance Co. in Fort Wayne, Indiana, was forming his own NASCAR team. He hired Isaac, who ran a partial slate in '67. The following year, the K&K Dodge team entered all the races and nearly won the title, finishing second to David Pearson. In 1969, Isaac won 17 races and earned 19 poles—the latter a single-season NASCAR Sprint Cup Series record.

The following year, Isaac and the K&K team jelled into one of stock car racing's most formidable combinations, winning 11 races and snaring the championship. Isaac went on to win five more races for Krauskopf's team, never again running a full schedule. In 1972, he suddenly quit the team.

Over the next four years, Isaac competed in a few NASCAR events, but he never won another race. In the twilight of his career, he was back in the saddle of a Sportsman car, competing weekly at his old Hickory Speedway stomping grounds. He died in August 1977.

During his big league NASCAR career, Isaac won 37 races in 307 starts, placing him 19th on the all-time win list. Through hard work and perseverance, he managed to elevate himself out of a world of poverty to become one of the most successful stock car drivers in the country.

Isaac drove the #71 K&K Insurance Dodge Daytona to 11 wins and the NASCAR championship in 1970.

Bobby Allison

After being runner-up in the championship race five times, Bobby Allison finally took home the trophy in 1983. His 84 NASCAR victories ties him for fourth on the all-time win list, and helped put him in the NASCAR Hall of Fame in 2011.

A brilliant driver for more than two decades, Bobby Allison became one of NASCAR's most prolific race winners. During his career, Allison won 84 races, tied for fourth in the all-time rankings. His greatest desire, however, was to win the elusive NASCAR championship.

In an era when General Motors cars were rendered noncompetitive in the face of the big-buck Ford and Chrysler factory efforts, Allison became a leader of the "little guys" and the unheralded "bow-tie brigade." The Hueytown, Alabama, driver won three times in 1966, then started attracting offers from top-ranked teams. During his career, Allison won races for a dozen different team owners and drove eight different makes of cars into Victory Lane.

Allison came close to winning the championship on a number of occasions. In 1970, he finished second to Bobby Isaac in the final points standings. He might have won but missed an early season race at Richmond because his short-track car wasn't finished in time. He came in second behind Richard Petty in 1972, despite leading in virtually every category: He had the most wins, won more poles than any other driver, led more than twice as many laps as any other driver, and led more races. He finished first or second in 22 of the 31 events. A season laced with excellence rewarded Allison with everything except that which he most wanted, the coveted driver's championship.

Three other runner-up finishes in the championship standings in 1978, '81, and '82 were bitter pills to swallow. "I've come so close so many times," said a discouraged Allison in '82. "Maybe I'm never going to win a Winston Cup championship."

But the following year, Allison's dream finally came true. "I've worked hard for a long, long time," he said after locking up the championship. "My wife Judy has worked with me, and so many people have supported me over the years. This is something I have wanted for my entire career and today I'm going to celebrate it. I just thank God for it."

Allison won the prestigious Daytona 500 three times. The last was in 1988, and it would prove to be the final victory of his driving career. Later that year, Allison was injured in a crash at Pocono. After a long recovery, he eventually returned to the NASCAR stage as a team owner.

Bobby Allison remains one of the greatest drivers ever to strap on a racing helmet, not only in NASCAR, but in any racing series. The fans adore his warm smile, his amiable attitude, and, most of all, his irrepressible spirit.

Left: *During his long NASCAR career, Bobby Allison won races in eight different makes of cars but drove a Buick through his 1983 championship season.*

Benny Parsons

Above: *After a rather inglorious introduction to NASCAR, Benny Parsons hit the big time with a championship in 1973 and a Daytona 500 victory in '75.*
Bottom right: *Parsons campaigned the #72 Chevrolet during his 1973 championship season.*

August 9, 1964. Asheville-Weaverville Speedway in the North Carolina mountains. A 250-mile race for NASCAR Sprint Cup Series drivers. The 45th of a record 62 NASCAR Sprint Cup Series races during the 1964 season.

Ford Motor Co., always on the lookout for a "diamond in the rough," summoned a couple of unheralded youngsters to audition for a factory-backed ride in the Asheville-Weaverville event. The two drivers Ford had their eye on were Cale Yarborough and Benny Parsons. It was the chance of a lifetime in auto racing's lifetime of chance. Both Yarborough and Parsons were strapped into potent '64 Ford Galaxies.

Yarborough put up an impressive performance, but Parsons did not. "I was just a kid and I didn't perform well," Parsons said years later. "It took me another six years to get into NASCAR racing."

Parsons's skill in stock cars netted him a pair of championships in the Automobile Racing Club of America. Another opportunity in NASCAR didn't come until 1969, and he didn't get a real shot at the big time until '70. Parsons was originally hired by L. G. DeWitt as a substitute driver for Buddy Young, who was injured in the '70 season opener at Riverside. While filling in, Parsons performed admirably, scoring 23 top-10 finishes in 45 starts in his rookie season. At the close of the year, DeWitt

elected to keep Parsons on the team's payroll.

Three years later, Parsons wore the crown as NASCAR Sprint Cup Series champion—against nearly impossible odds. The DeWitt team had no sponsorship during the 1973 season. Their racing arsenal contained only three cars while most of the top contenders had a full fleet of machinery at their disposal.

Parsons's NASCAR Sprint Cup career continued through the 1988 season. In addition to his title season in '73, he captured NASCAR's biggest event, the Daytona 500, in '75. He logged 21 victories in stock car racing's premier series and was voted among the top 50 drivers in NASCAR history during the Golden Anniversary in 1998.

After his retirement, Parsons went into television commentary. He served as an analyst for NASCAR Sprint Cup Series broadcasts starting in 1989 and remained a fan favorite until he died of complications from cancer treatment in 2007.

After his retirement from racing, Benny Parsons became a NASCAR commentator, adding colorful insight to the broadcasts.

Darrell Waltrip

Above: *In a miraculous reversal of image, Darrell Waltrip went from disliked bad boy to fan favorite—somewhat* after *winning three NASCAR championships. In 2012, he was inducted into the NASCAR Hall of Fame.* **Right:** *Waltrip drove the #11 Buick to his first championship in 1981.*

Darrell Waltrip was one of short-track racing's flashiest speed artists during his ascent from weekly bullrings to the glamorous stage of NASCAR racing. Armed with a positive attitude, supreme self-confidence, and some of the finest machinery in the weekly short track wars in the Tennessee-Kentucky area, Waltrip established an enviable portfolio in the late 1960s and early '70s.

In 1973, Waltrip joined the NASCAR tour full time. In a matter of months, Waltrip gained a reputation as a very capable driver, but one who ruffled plenty of feathers. He barged into prominence with his mouth running as fast as his race cars. His words often earned the wrath of trackside spectators, who responded with a chorus of boos when he was introduced before a race.

Over the years, however, Waltrip matured and became a championship-caliber driver. He joined forces with former-driver-turned-team-owner Junior Johnson in 1981, and the combination clicked. Waltrip won his first NASCAR championship, and repeated the feat in 1982. In '85, he won the title for a third time.

During his championship reign, Waltrip was still one of the most disliked drivers in the NASCAR kingdom. But all that changed on May 21, 1989, at Charlotte Motor Speedway during the running of NASCAR's fifth annual NASCAR Sprint All-Star Race. Waltrip was running first as he approached the white flag when second-place driver Rusty Wallace hit the rear of Waltrip's Chevy, spinning him out. Wallace went on to victory, and Waltrip publicly stated, "I hope he chokes on that $200,000 [winner's prize]. He drove into me and spun me out. It was pretty flagrant."

In an instant, Waltrip went from disliked bad boy to a popular champion. And in a correspondingly odd turn of events, Waltrip was voted NASCAR's Most Popular Driver in 1989 and 1990 by NASCAR fans.

During his storied 1972–2000 NASCAR career, Waltrip won 84 races, tied for fourth on the all-time list. After his retirement from racing, Waltrip further enhanced his public image as a racing analyst, adding a touch of Southern charm to NASCAR Sprint Cup Series telecasts.

Below: *After his retirement from racing, Waltrip became a TV commentator for NASCAR events.*

Dale Earnhardt

Dale Earnhardt's aggressive driving style earned him his nickname: "The Intimidator." He tied Richard Petty's record of seven NASCAR championships, but a tragedy-shortened career took away his chance of winning an eighth. He posthumously became an inaugural inductee into the NASCAR Hall of Fame in 2010.

November 5, 1978, was a pivotal day in Dale Earnhardt's racing career. After running several NASCAR events in noncompetitive cars, Earnhardt got his first real ride that day in the Dixie 500 at Atlanta Motor Speedway.

The strapping son of the legendary Ralph Earnhardt was seated in a Chevrolet fielded by Osterlund Racing. Earnhardt drove the Osterlund car for all it was worth, finishing fourth after starting 10th.

That led to a full-time ride with Osterlund's team for the 1979 season. After nearly winning the Daytona 500, Earnhardt won the Southeastern 500 at Bristol and came in a close second in the Dixie 500 at Atlanta on his way to winning the Sunoco Rookie of the Year award.

In 1980, Earnhardt made history. He took the lead in the points standings shortly after the Daytona 500 and never relinquished his grip on first place. No other driver had won the Sunoco Rookie of the Year award and the championship in back-to-back seasons.

After signing on with the Richard Childress team in 1981, Earnhardt continued his winning ways, though his second championship eluded him until 1986. The following year, he thoroughly dominated the NASCAR Sprint Cup Series season, taking his third title. He went on to rack up cham-

pionships in 1990, '91, '93, and '94, tying Richard Petty with seven titles. Always a hard charger, Earnhardt earned the nickname "The Intimidator" for his aggressive, sometimes bullying driving style.

After enduring a bit of a slump in the late 1990s, Earnhardt appeared back at the top of his game by the turn of the century. He finished second in the 2000 NASCAR Sprint Cup Series points standings and was eagerly awaiting the start of the 2001 campaign, where he would have had a strong shot at a record eighth NASCAR Sprint Cup Series title.

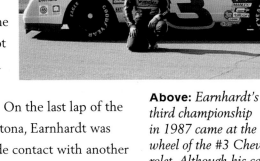

But his shot never came. On the last lap of the 2001 season opener at Daytona, Earnhardt was running third when he made contact with another car and lost control. He slid into the concrete retaining barrier, and the angle of the impact was such that it dealt a fatal blow to one of NASCAR's most popular drivers.

Earnhardt's death sparked controversy, resulting in NASCAR tightening its safety regulations. All drivers are now required to wear the HANS device, a head and neck support collar designed to prevent sudden forward movement of a driver's head in the event of a frontal impact.

Above: *Earnhardt's third championship in 1987 came at the wheel of the #3 Chevrolet. Although his cars carried other numbers early in his career, "Earnhardt" and "3" eventually became synonymous.* **Bottom:** *Another #3 Chevrolet carried Earnhardt to his fifth championship in 1991.*

Bill Elliott

Above: *He won the NASCAR championship in 1988, but Bill Elliott may be best remembered for his record-setting qualifying speeds at Daytona (below) and Talladega, which he circled at more than 212 mph.*

After more than three decades on the NASCAR circuit, Bill Elliott has all but retired from competing in the NASCAR Sprint Cup Series. It's not as though he has anything to prove: With one championship and several records under his belt, Elliott has certainly earned his place in NASCAR history.

For the first seven years of his NASCAR career, Elliott ran only a partial schedule. Though he failed to reach Victory Lane, he did record 10 top-five finishes. He first raced full time in 1983, the year he also earned his first victory.

He added three more in '84, then exploded in '85 with a career-high 11 wins. He also won the inaugural Winston Million that year, a one-million-dollar award paid to any driver who could win three out of the four top races of the season (the Daytona 500, Winston 500, Coca-Cola 600, and Southern 500). This feat earned him the nick-name "Million Dollar Bill" and also helped make him the first NASCAR driver to grace the cover of *Sports Illustrated* magazine.

After finishing second in the points standings in 1985, fourth in '86, and second again in '87, Elliott finally won the championship in 1988.

But history might best remember him for his 1987 season, when he not only set the all-time top qualifying speed of 212.809 mph at Talladega, but also set the top qualifying speed of 210.364 mph at Daytona International Speedway. Because NASCAR responded to these frightening speeds by requiring cars to run restrictor plates at both of those tracks—where nobody has since reached 200 mph in qualifying—Elliott's records will likely never be broken.

The #9 Thunderbird Elliott campaigned in 1987 is—and probably always will be—the fastest car ever to qualify for a NASCAR Sprint Cup Series event.

Though Elliott never won a second championship, he was runner-up in 1992, missing the mark by just 10 points. Thereafter he never placed higher than 8th but did manage to add five more wins to his total, which stands at 44.

Besides his 1988 championship and two qualifying-speed records, the soft-spoken man from Dawsonville, Georgia, will also be remembered for receiving NASCAR's Most Popular Driver Award 16 times, most recently in 2002, after which he removed his name from the ballot. He was inducted into the NASCAR Hall of Fame in 2015.

Terry Labonte

Above: *Terry Labonte began his NASCAR career in 1978 and won his first championship in 1984 driving the #44 Peidmont Airlines Chevrolet* **(below).**

In the summer of 1978, Terry Labonte was driving NASCAR Sportsman cars on the short tracks in and around his hometown of Corpus Christi, Texas. In August, NASCAR team owner Billy Hagan, who had just released 1976 Sunoco Rookie of the Year Skip Manning, decided to give the 22-year-old kid a shot at the big time.

Darlington's Southern 500 was the next race on the annual NASCAR Sprint Cup Series calendar. Eerie Darlington, with a personality akin to an angry pit bull, was hardly the place for a green rookie to attempt his first big-league start. "I had never even seen Darlington before I went there in 1978," said Labonte. While taking a maiden voyage at Darlington would be challenging, Labonte was up to the task. Driving the Hagan Chevrolet, Labonte was smooth, steady, and fast. Most importantly, he didn't flinch in the face of Darlington's fearsome reputation. The Texas hotshot finished an amazing fourth.

Two years later, Labonte was back at Darlington for the 1980 Southern 500. Starting 10th on the grid, Labonte again quietly and effectively drove into contention. Throughout the 500-miler, Labonte

managed to keep his car on the lead lap. Near the end of the race, Labonte, running at full stride, dove low and passed David Pearson a couple of feet before the stripe. He beat Pearson back to the caution flag by less than two feet to secure his first NASCAR Sprint Cup Series victory as the race ended under yellow.

With his signature steady driving, Labonte became a contender for the championship by his third full season. He finished fourth in 1981, third in '82, and fifth in '83. In 1984, Labonte overtook Dale Earnhardt for the points lead in August and drove to his first NASCAR Sprint Cup Series title. He won two races during the run.

A dozen years later, Labonte drove to his second NASCAR championship as a member of the Hendrick Motorsports team. He and teammate Jeff Gordon engaged in a stirring points battle during the final stretch of the 1996 season. With three races remaining, Labonte overtook Gordon and edged his stablemate by a mere 37 points.

Labonte set another mark in 1996. With his April 21 start at Martinsville, Labonte broke Richard Petty's record of 513 consecutive starts. The streak extended into 2000 when he made his 655th consecutive NASCAR Sprint Cup Series start at Daytona in July, but ended when he had to miss the August 5 race at Indianapolis. Labonte's streak, which started in 1979, was surpassed by Ricky Rudd in 2002.

Labonte retired from full-time NASCAR Sprint Cup Series competition after the 2004 season, but he continues to run a few races each year.

Above and below: *Twelve years after scoring his first championship, Labonte earned his second at the wheel of the #5 Kellogg's Chevrolet in 1996. He has amassed 22 wins and continues to race part-time in a NASCAR Sprint Cup Series career that now spans more than three decades.*

Rusty Wallace

Above and right:
Rusty Wallace won the NASCAR Sprint Cup Series championship in 1989 wheeling the #27 Pontiac. He was inducted into the NASCAR Hall of Fame in 2013.

Born Russell William Wallace in 1956, "Rusty" began racing at smaller tracks near his Missouri home in the late 1970s. After winning a couple of local championships, he captured the United States Auto Club (USAC) Rookie of the Year award in 1979 and the American Speed Association (ASA) championship four years later.

In his very first NASCAR race at the Atlanta 500 in 1980, Rusty drove his Chevrolet to a second-place finish, taking the checkered flag just 10 seconds behind winner Dale Earnhardt—an amazing feat for a rookie driver. After just a handful of starts in '81 and '82, and none in '83, Rusty began racing on the NASCAR circuit full time in 1984. He scored his first win in the Valleydale 500 at Bristol in 1986 and added a second that year at the Goody's 500 in Martinsville. He scored two more wins during the '87 season, then went on a tear: six victories in 1988, when he came in second behind Bill Elliott in the championship race, and six more in '89, when he came in second to no one. After his championship season, Rusty added two wins each in 1990 and '91, and one more in 1992.

But in many ways, Rusty's best years were yet to come. He managed a career-high 10 wins in 1993, when he was runner-up to Earnhardt for the championship. His eight victories the following year left him third in the championship race.

Rusty scored 15 more wins from 1995 to 2002, and though he never won another championship, he was in the top 10 in points every year.

Rusty won his final race in 2004 at Martinsville Speedway. Later that year he announced that 2005 would be his last full season, and his last year on the NASCAR Sprint Cup Series circuit. Though many drivers of his status race part-time before fading away completely, Rusty wasn't planning on fading away just yet.

During the 2006 race season, Rusty covered the IndyCar Series open-wheel racing as a television announcer for The Walt Disney Company networks, where his assignments included coverage of the prestigious Indianapolis 500. The following year, he began covering NASCAR events for ABC and ESPN.

Besides his broadcasting gig, Rusty also ran Rusty Wallace, Inc., which campaigned two cars in the NASCAR Nationwide Series, one of which was driven by his son, Steve Wallace.

Bottom left: *In 2004, Wallace scored the last of his 55 NASCAR victories in the #2 Dodge at Martinsville. The following year, he waved to fans during the parade lap at Bristol (below).*

Mark Martin

Sometimes referred to as "the best driver to never win a championship," Mark Martin has been runner-up five times and amassed an impressive 40 career victories.

Mark Martin is one of the most successful drivers on the NASCAR circuit, a focused veteran who over his long career has earned the admiration and respect of fans and competitors alike.

Born in Batesville, Arkansas, on January 9, 1959, Martin was already a formidable competitor around Arkansas's dirt tracks by the time he got his driver's license. He then moved on to ASA (American Speed Association) racing, where he soon dominated. He was named the ASA's Rookie of the Year in 1977 while still in high school. From 1978 to 1980, he won three consecutive ASA titles.

Martin first made the jump to NASCAR in 1981, winning a couple of poles and finishing in the top 10 twice while fielding his own team. In spite of this promising start, Martin was woefully underfunded against established competitors and struggled through the 1982 season. After a short-lived stint with team owner J. D. Stacy and a few part-time rides with low-budget teams during the 1983 season, Martin returned to ASA, winning a fourth championship in 1986.

Rebounding from his discouraging early NASCAR forays, Martin joined freshman team owner Jack Roush in 1988. The pair clicked, and their relationship would prove to be one of the longest-running and most successful driver/owner pairings in NASCAR history.

Martin's first NASCAR win was the 1989 AC Delco 500 in Rockingham. "My life is fulfilled," he said after the victory. Little did he know that his life was about to get much more fulfilling.

From there, Martin went on to amass an impressive record, but one goal remained achingly elusive: a NASCAR championship. In 1990, Martin finished second in the standings, a mere 26 points behind champion Dale Earnhardt. More heartbreaking was the fact that Martin's team was penalized 46 points at Richmond for running a carburetor spacer that was a half-inch too thick. As it turned out, the penalty cost him the championship. Martin would be runner-up in the points standings four more times—in 1994, 1998, 2002, and 2009—but never snagged NASCAR's ultimate crown.

But as he has continuously shown, Martin is not deterred by setbacks. His disciplined lifestyle, which includes a strict physical-fitness regimen, has made him a more focused competitor. Martin finally left Roush Fenway Racing after the 2006 season so he could run a reduced schedule with Ginn Racing and later Dale Earnhardt, Inc., but he returned as a full-time driver for Hendrick Motorsports for the 2009-2011 seasons. Martin drove part time for a couple more seasons, but at an age when most drivers had long since retired. After the 2013 season, he finally hung up his helmet.

> "I don't like getting upside down, and I was fixin' to."
>
> —Mark Martin after getting airborne and nearly flipping in the 1991 Winston 500 at Talladega

Martin enjoyed some of his best years at the wheel of the #6 Valvoline Ford.

Dale Jarrett

Above: *Dale Jarrett is the son of 1961/'65 NASCAR champion Ned Jarrett and, in 1999, added another championship trophy to the family treasure chest. He drove the #88 Ford* (top right) *to four wins that year. In 2014, he joined his father in the NASCAR Hall of Fame.*

Dale Jarrett grew up around North Carolina's Hickory Speedway, a .363-mile oval managed by his father, NASCAR racing great Ned Jarrett. Dale began his career in the mid 1970s competing at Hickory and other weekly tracks. From there he moved up the racing ranks, and finally got a few one-shot deals in NASCAR's top series beginning in 1984, landing a full-time assignment by '87. Success was again slow in coming, as Jarrett managed only two top-five finishes in his first 110 starts.

In 1991, after a lengthy apprenticeship driving for the Woods Brothers Ford team, Jarrett finally began to reap rewards, scoring his first victory that year at Michigan. It wasn't until '93 that he recorded his second win, but it was a big one: the prestigious Daytona 500. The victory was especially sweet because his father, Ned, was one of the commentators covering the race for CBS Sports.

After three years with the Gibbs operation, Jarrett moved over to the Robert Yates camp in 1995. He won once that year, then captured his second Daytona 500 in the '96 season opener. A few months later, he drove home first in the Brickyard 400, and thus won the two biggest prizes of the annual NASCAR calendar.

Jarrett was a serious championship contender in 1996, finishing third on the strength of four victories. He came in a close second to Jeff Gordon

in the '97 points race, took third in '98, and finally grabbed the crown after a sparkling season in '99. Jarrett nabbed the points lead after the 11th race of the season in May and never looked back. "The championship is my greatest accomplishment," he reflected. "I'm prouder of that than anything else."

When Dale captured NASCAR's most cherished prize, the Jarrett racing family became only the second father-and-son combination to win the NASCAR championship. (The first was Lee and Richard Petty.)

Jarrett's prowess on NASCAR's speedy stage continued into the 21st century. He captured his third Daytona 500 win in 2000, was in contention for the championship both that year and the next, and won at least one race every season from 1993 to 2003. After his retirement in 2008 at the age of 51, Jarrett went on to become a NASCAR commentator for ESPN.

Below: *Jarrett's final competitive drive was in the 2008 NASCAR Sprint All-Star Race at Charlotte Motor Speedway. It was an emotional end to a memorable quarter-century NASCAR career.*

Alan Kulwicki

Running his privately owned team with comparatively little support, Alan Kulwicki surprised nearly everyone by winning the 1992 NASCAR championship. Sadly, his bright future as a driver and team owner was cut tragically short.

Alan Kulwicki, an underdog from Greenfield, Wisconsin, produced NASCAR's most unlikely championship run during the 1992 NASCAR Sprint Cup Series season. He overcame the greatest late-season deficit in championship history and, along the way, gave hope to every small-time operator in NASCAR.

Kulwicki began the 1992 NASCAR season as one of the dozens of drivers with seemingly no realistic shot at NASCAR's most elusive prize. As an owner, driver, bookkeeper, and strategist, Kulwicki faced an uphill battle against the heavily funded and established teams.

On the strength of consistent finishes and a couple of victories during the spring and summer, Kulwicki clambered into contention.

Entering the season finale at Atlanta, six drivers had a shot at the championship. Kulwicki was only 30 points behind points leader Davey Allison and 10 points ahead of Bill Elliott. One of the most dynamic duels in the history of the title chase unfolded that afternoon at Atlanta Motor Speedway.

Allison's title hopes were dashed when he crashed midway through the race. With that, there was a distinct possibility that for the first time in history, a tiebreaker would be used to determine the NASCAR Sprint Cup Series champion.

For much of the contest, Elliott and Kulwicki ran first and second, swapping the lead. Because Elliott started the race 10 points behind, he not only needed the five points that separated first and second place, but also the five points awarded to the driver who led the most laps. That would leave the two drivers in a tie, and Elliott, by virtue of

leading Kulwicki 4-2 in wins for the season, held the tiebreaker.

Toward the end of the race, Kulwicki was leading but needed to pit for fuel. He and his crew chief, Paul Andrews, figured out exactly how many laps Kulwicki needed to stay in front in order to earn the five points for leading the most laps. Kulwicki managed to stretch his fuel to hit that mark, and though Elliott won the race, Kulwicki won the championship.

Kulwicki's title run in 1992 was one for the ages. It proved that with determination, hard work, intelligence, and a little luck, a small-time operator could rise to the pinnacle of his profession.

In 1993, Kulwicki had begun his title defense in solid fashion, scoring three top-10 finishes and holding down ninth in the points standings. Following an appearance in Knoxville, Tennessee, Kulwicki was flying to Bristol for the Food City 500 when the company plane crashed into a meadow near Blountville, Tennessee. The lives of Kulwicki, Mark Brooks, Dan Duncan, and pilot Charlie Campbell were lost. The champion wouldn't have the chance to defend his title.

> "Obstacles are what you see when you take your eyes off the goal line."

Kulwicki nicknamed his #7 Ford Thunderbird the "Underbird" due to the fact he was going into the 1992 title chase as a decided underdog.

Jeff Gordon

Jeff Gordon started racing at an early age and, at 24, netted his first of four NASCAR championships in just his second full season.

Before he was old enough to drive on public roads, Jeffrey Michael Gordon had won two national Quarter Midget championships, four go-kart championships, and several races in the All Star Circuit of Champions Sprint Car series.

"When I was five years old," reflected Gordon, "it was just something my dad did to keep me out of my mom's way and give me something to do in the field near our house. For most of my life, racing was what we did for fun on weekends."

The climb to racing's major leagues was orchestrated by Jeff's stepfather John Bickford. At 16, Gordon became the youngest recipient of a United States Auto Club competitor's license. In 1989, Gordon won races in three USAC open-wheel divisions, graduated from high school, and became a full-time race car driver. After successful seasons in Midget and Sprint Car racing, Gordon landed a ride with Bill Davis's team in the NASCAR Nationwide Series. "My focus for the future is NASCAR racing," Gordon said at the time. "I'm in stock cars to stay. For me, NASCAR racing holds the greatest promise and potential."

It wasn't long before he caught the eye of NASCAR Sprint Cup Series team owner Rick Hendrick, who quickly signed him to a multiyear contract. Gordon took Sunoco Rookie of the Year honors in 1993 and won two big races the following year: the Coca-Cola 600

and the inaugural Brickyard 400 at Indianapolis Motor Speedway.

In 1995, Gordon snared his first NASCAR championship at the age of 24, becoming the second youngest man to ever cop NASCAR's most cherished crown. He won the championship again in 1997 and '98. His fourth championship came in 2001, making him one of only four drivers in history to win more than three NASCAR Sprint Cup Series titles.

Time will tell if Gordon is able to match or surpass the record of seven championships jointly held by legends Richard Petty and Dale Earnhardt. This much is certain, though: Jeff Gordon shines brightly among NASCAR's biggest stars.

Above: *In 1997 at the age of 25, Gordon became the youngest driver ever to win the Daytona 500.* **Below:** *Chevrolet and the #24 have both become synonymous with Gordon.*

Dale Earnhardt, Jr.

The son of one of the most famous drivers in NASCAR history, Dale Earnhardt Jr. will probably always be known simply as "Junior." To date, he has won the Most Popular Driver Award 11 years running.

Dale Earnhardt, Jr., is both blessed and burdened with one of the most legendary names in stock car racing history. As the son of the late NASCAR icon Dale Earnhardt, Dale Jr. has inherited his father's instincts and hard-charging driving style. Because he is his father's son and the heir to a great racing legacy, he usually operates under greater media and public scrutiny.

Usually referred to as "Junior," Earnhardt, Jr., began his professional racing career at 17, competing in the street stock division at Concord Motorsport Park, a half-mile tri-oval track near his Kannapolis, North Carolina, hometown. He then moved up to the NASCAR Nationwide Series, where he soon dominated with back-to-back championships in 1998 and '99. He also ran five NASCAR Sprint Cup Series events in '99 before moving to NASCAR's top series full time in 2000. Junior quickly made a name for himself, capturing two wins and two poles during his rookie season.

Tragedy struck Earnhardt Jr.'s life in 2001 when his father, Dale Earnhardt Sr., died from injuries sustained during the Daytona 500. But Junior stood tall in the face of this immense loss, scoring an emotional Daytona victory five months later at the Pepsi 400 and winning twice more to finish eighth in the 2001 standings.

The 2003 season saw Junior become a true title contender as he scored a record-breaking fourth consecutive win at Talladega on his way to a career-best third-place finish in the final standings. In 2004, Earnhardt, Jr., conquered Daytona again, winning the Daytona 500 on his way to a career-high six victories and a fifth-place finish.

In spite of an intense personal schedule, Earnhardt, Jr., maintains a laid-back demeanor and an ability to cut loose and have a good time. Recalling his days as a mechanic in his dad's Chevrolet dealership, he also enjoys working on his extensive specialty-car collection.

Over the course of his racing career, Earnhardt, Jr., has become a *bona fide* mainstream celebrity. In addition to the expected barrage of advertising and promotional appearances, he has appeared on TV talk shows, in MTV and VH-1 documentaries, in Hollywood movies, and in music videos, as well as in several popular magazines such as *People, Maxim, Forbes,* and *Rolling Stone.* He is an 11-time-consecutive winner of the National Motorsports Press Association's Most Popular Driver award. As a third-generation stock car driver, Dale Earnhardt, Jr., represents NASCAR's southern past and its future. His 2014 Daytona 500 win broke a 55-race dry spell.

Junior drove his #8 Chevrolet to his first NASCAR Sprint Cup Series victory in the DirecTV 500 at Texas Motor Speedway.

Tony Stewart

Tony Stewart's quick rise in the NASCAR ranks isn't surprising given his extensive racing history in various types of cars. In fact, he has been known to run both an IndyCar Series event and a NASCAR Sprint Cup Series event on the same day. Stewart already has three NASCAR championships to his credit and continues to be a formidable competitor.

Tony Stewart's rookie season in 1999 was one of the most eventful in the history of NASCAR racing. The 27-year-old from Columbus, Indiana, finished fourth overall in the championship chase on the strength of three wins (all in the season's second half), 12 top-five finishes, and 21 top-10 showings. On May 30, he raced in two events on the same day, finishing ninth in the IndyCar Series' Indianapolis 500 and fourth in NASCAR's Coca-Cola 600 at Charlotte Motor Speedway. He reprised this jaw-dropping feat in 2001, bettering his 1999 showing by finishing sixth in the Indy 500 and third in the 600-miler.

In 2002, Stewart rallied from a last-place finish in the season-opening Daytona 500, scrambled back into contention, and delivered a late-season kick to capture the 2002 NASCAR championship. He nabbed the championship again in 2005 after racking up five wins, and made it a hat trick in 2011, when he also scored five wins. At the end of the 2013 NASCAR season, Stewart had an impressive 48 wins to his credit.

Stewart's quick success in NASCAR's top series is not surprising given his racing history. He cut his teeth on kart racing at a young age, snagging his first championship title when he was eight years old. He moved up the open-wheel ranks to three-quarter midgets and then on to the USAC (United States Auto Club) series. In 1995, he became the first driver to sweep the USAC Midget, Sprint Car, and Silver Crown championships. In 1996, Stewart entered the newly formed IRL (Indy Racing

League), where he claimed the Rookie of the Year title and followed that up with the IRL championship. Stewart hooked up with Joe Gibbs Racing in 1997, running in the NASCAR Nationwide Series before moving with Gibbs to NASCAR's top level of competition. Prior to the 2009 season, Stewart became co-owner of his own team.

Stewart's NASCAR career has been undeniably successful but also volatile, with a notable number of scuffles with other drivers and trackside photographers. This hot-tempered personality has earned Tony a bit of a "bad boy" reputation, as well as some punitive fines from NASCAR officials. Stewart's positive emotions are equally unrestrained. Along with the rest of NASCAR's "young guns," Stewart has brought a new level of boisterous showmanship to the traditional NASCAR victory celebration with his smoke-billowing burnouts and fence-climbing escapades.

Stewart's public persona was shattered in 2014 following a fatal accident in a sprint-car race. A local driver was struck and killed by the right rear tire of Stewart's car as the driver tried to confront Stewart. Stewart sat out three races in the aftermath of the tragedy and was cleared of any wrongdoing by an official NASCAR investigation.

Stewart wheeled the #20 Home Depot Pontiac to his first championship in 2002.

Jimmie Johnson

In 2009, Jimmie Johnson became the first driver to win four consecutive NASCAR Sprint Cup Series championships, finally topping Cale Yarborough's long-standing record. He added to that by winning a fifth straight in 2010, and then took his sixth championship in 2013. Johnson's credentials also include victories in the Daytona 500 and NASCAR Sprint All-Star Race.

Unlike most of his contemporaries, Jimmie Kenneth Johnson arrived at NASCAR racing the old-fashioned way: via the dirt. While he didn't run the dusty oval tracks that groomed many drivers of the '40s and '50s, he was on dirt all the same.

Born September 17, 1975, in El Cajon, California, Johnson began riding off-road bikes at the age of five and won a 60-cc championship three years later. In his teens, he moved to four-wheeled machines, eventually winning more than 25 stadium and desert races on the way to six championships in three leagues, earning Rookie of the Year honors in each of them.

It wasn't until 1998 that Johnson got his first taste of competition on pavement. He joined the American Speed Association, where he finished fourth in the standings in his freshman year and took home yet another Rookie of the Year trophy. He also dabbled in the NASCAR Nationwide Series, competing in three races.

Johnson continued to run both ASA and NASCAR Nationwide Series events in 1999 before becoming a full-time NASCAR Nationwide driver in 2000. He then moved up to NASCAR's premier series when he signed a driver development deal with Hendrick Motorsports.

In his first full year of NASCAR Sprint Cup Series competition in 2002, Johnson amassed an impressive record. His first win came in the NAPA Auto Parts 500 at Auto Club Speedway and was followed by two more that same year.

Johnson racked up another three victories in 2003 and also won the NASCAR Sprint All-Star Race, a non-points-race event. He finished the season in second place, 90 points behind Matt Kenseth.

Despite amassing eight wins in 2004—the most of any driver—Johnson once again came in second in what was the closest finish in NASCAR Sprint Cup Series history. The season now ended with the ten-race Chase for the NASCAR Sprint Cup, and Johnson finished just eight points behind Kurt Busch.

By contrast, 2005 was almost a lackluster year for Johnson as he ended up fifth in the standings.

Johnson started off the 2006 season with a bang, winning the opening Daytona 500. This was followed by four more victories—along with a win at the NASCAR Sprint All-Star Race—and at the end of the season, he beat Kenseth by 56 points to become the 2006 NASCAR Sprint Cup champion.

Johnson continued his winning ways in 2007. After winning 10 races, he finished the season 77 points ahead of teammate Jeff Gordon to win his second straight title.

Good as Johnson's luck had been, it was about to get even better. In 2008, he won seven races and his third championship in a row. In so doing, Johnson tied the record of Cale Yarborough, the first—and previously, only—driver to win three consecutive championships, having done so in 1976-1978. Johnson came back in 2009 to win a record-setting four consecutive championships, then made it five straight by winning it again in 2010. He added his sixth in 2013, showing no sign of slowing down.

Since his first full NASCAR Sprint Cup Series season in 2002, Johnson's car has always been a Chevrolet, and it's always worn a florescent-green "48" on its flanks.

CHAPTER TWO

THE CARS

In the first NASCAR Strictly Stock race in 1949, the cars had to be just that: strictly stock. Today, they're anything but. The transformation from showroom siblings to dedicated racing machines was gradual, though it began almost immediately. Safety was the primary reason behind the first modifications that were allowed—and often mandated—as cars built for the street couldn't be expected to handle the stress of a racing environment. But perhaps the biggest changes came when Detroit made a move to front-wheel-drive cars in the mid-1980s, necessitating that specially built bodies that looked somewhat stock be mounted on purpose-built racing chassis. Then came "equalized" body shells for consistent aerodynamics and eventually today's design, which has leveled the playing field and made for close competition.

Hudson was one of the first manufacturers to offer hot-rod versions of production cars for competition, and also one of the first to promote its NASCAR victories in advertisements.

1948

NASCAR's first sanctioned race was held in February 1948 at the famed Daytona Beach & Road Course in Daytona Beach, Florida. It featured Modifieds, which were normal street cars that had been stripped down and souped up to make them faster at the tracks. Because new cars were still in short supply due to curtailed production during World War II, most Modifieds were prewar cars—primarily Fords, with their powerful flathead V-8s.

Left: *A flock of prewar Fords battle in the NASCAR Modified Division. Fords were chosen by the bulk of competitors due to their potent flathead V-8s.*

Above and below: *By the time Modifieds were modified, it was sometimes difficult to tell what make of car they had been in the first place.*

1949–1951

After holding a pair of trial 10-mile Strictly Stock Late Model competitions in early 1949, NASCAR ran the first Strictly Stock (now NASCAR Sprint Cup Series) race in June 1949: a 150-mile event at the ¾-mile Charlotte Speedway. As the series name implied, the cars had to be showroom stock—no modifications allowed. A Ford crossed the finish line first, but the car was later disqualified for having stiffer-than-stock rear springs, and the victory was awarded to a Lincoln. In subsequent events, however, Oldsmobile's speedy new 88 with its Rocket V-8 engine was the car of choice, winning 35 of 68 races over the next three years.

Above: *Oldsmobile's powerful overhead-valve Rocket V-8 engine introduced for 1949 gave the make's lightweight 88 (top right) a distinct advantage in NASCAR's new Strictly Stock division.*

Far left: *Lincolns made a strong showing in '49 and '50 with their big flathead V-8s, but the cars cost more than comparable Oldsmobiles. During the same period, lowly flathead-six Plymouths (left) did surprisingly well, partly due to their light weight and sturdy construction.*

Right: *The Strictly Stock division attracted a vast number of makes, which was part of the appeal—as was the fact the cars were "showroom stock." The starting grid at the first Strictly Stock race shows an Olds on the "pole" with a Ford on the outside, followed by a Hudson, Buick, earlier Ford, and a Kaiser.*

1952-1954

Right and far right:
Hudson's Hornet began making an impact on NASCAR as soon as it was introduced in 1951 but really hit its stride in '52–'54. A huge, potent flathead six and corner-hugging Step-Down construction made it a race track terror, a fact not lost on Hudson's marketing department.

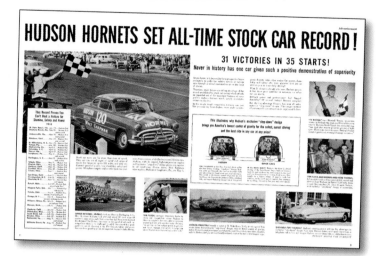

Starting in 1952, NASCAR began awarding an annual Manufacturers Championship. The points system for it has changed over the years, but it's always been based on finishing positions rather than just wins. Therefore, the make claiming the most victories doesn't always win the championship, just as the driver with the most wins doesn't always take the NASCAR Sprint Cup Series championship.

Oldsmobile's dominance in stock car competition was brought to an end by an unlikely rival: the flathead-six-powered Hudson Hornet. But the high-performance Twin-H Power engine wasn't any ordinary flathead six, and the Hornet wasn't any ordinary car; its Step-Down construction (the body sat between the frame rails rather than on top of them) created a lower center of gravity that resulted in class-leading handling. Oldsmobiles still won a fair number of races as did several other makes, but Hudsons took 66 of 112 events during the 1952–54 time frame and won the Manufacturers Championship each of those years.

Left: *Dodge introduced a small Hemi V-8 engine for 1953, and not coincidentally, the make won its first NASCAR race that year. In fact, Dodges came home first in six events during 1953, the only make besides Hudson and Olds to score a win.* **Below:** *A bigger Rocket V-8 kept Oldsmobiles in the hunt in '54.*

1955-1956

You get the winning V8 in Chevrolet!

Above: *A pair of Chrysler 300s lead an Olds in a 1955 race. Although Chryslers posted the most wins that year, Oldsmobile won the Manufacturers' Championship—mostly because more drivers could afford the $2500 Olds than the $4100 Chrysler 300.*

Right and top right: *Chevrolets got a potent overhead-valve V-8 for 1955 that helped them to their first NASCAR wins—victories that were pointed out in the company's ads.*

Right: *Fords also got an overhead-valve V-8—and a couple of NASCAR victories—for 1955, and a larger version of the engine in '56 gave the company 14 wins and the Manufacturers' Championship.*

When Chrysler brought out its advanced Hemi V-8 for 1951, it seemed only a matter of time before it would take the stock car circuit by storm. That finally happened in 1955–56, when Chryslers won 49 of 101 events and Hemi-powered Dodges added another 12. Nevertheless, Chrysler didn't win the Manufacturers' Championship in either year. The 1955 award went to Oldsmobile, despite the fact that it won only 10 races to Chrysler's 27. Both Chevrolet and Ford introduced modern overhead-valve V-8s that year that made them competitive with the more-expensive makes that traditionally dominated NASCAR events, and Ford took the 1956 championship. Former champion Hudson was flat out-gunned, winning only one race during this period.

Below: *Five Mercurys crossed the finish line first in 1956, but this wasn't one of them. Russ Trulove tumbled his race car but walked away unscathed.*

1957–1958

Chevrolet and Pontiac introduced fuel-injected V-8s for 1957 while Ford offered supercharging, but NASCAR moved quickly to ban both. Rules were written to allow only normally aspirated carbureted engines, and despite subsequent advances in technology, those rules remain in effect to this day.

Top and below: *Ford and Chevy were the biggest winners in the 1957–58 time frame.*

Below: *Car companies weren't the only ones to find advertising fodder in racing. Firestone aimed to boost its image by trumpeting its achievements in the "Oval Laboratory."*

Fords won 26 of 53 races in 1957—along with the Manufacturers' Championship—while Chevys were victorious in 21. The two makes swapped positions and titles in '58, when Chevy took home the trophy in 25 of 51 races, and Ford won another 16. It was during this time that the Automobile Manufacturers Association (AMA) announced that factory support of racing would be suspended due to fears that speeds on the track were adversely affecting safety on the streets, making lower-priced cars more attractive to teams.

1959-1960

Above: *Although no longer the dominating force they once were, Oldsmobiles won four races in 1959, most notably the inaugural Daytona 500 with Lee Petty at the wheel.*

Chevrolets and Fords again dominated NASCAR competition in 1959 with 16 wins each, with Chevy netting the Manufacturers' Championship. Plymouths made their mark by scoring seven victories. Fords took the checkered flag 15 times in 1960 vs. 13 for Chevrolet, yet Chevy won the championship again. Meanwhile, Plymouth garnered eight wins and a surging Pontiac took seven. The only other makes to score wins during the 1959–60 time frame were Oldsmobile (four) and Dodge (one).

1961-1962

Pontiacs ran rampant in 1961, winning 30 of 52 NASCAR races, yet Chevrolet won the Manufacturers' Championship with just 11 victories. Ford had seven, while Plymouth and Chrysler took home a combined four. Things evened out a bit for 1962, with 22 victories—and the championship—for Pontiac, 14 for Chevy, 11 for Plymouth, and six for Ford. A notable transformation began in 1962 when Dodge and Plymouth bucked the established longer/lower/wider trend by "downsizing" their redesigned full-size cars. Both makes eventually brought out larger models but continued to race what had become intermediates. By 1967, intermediate GMs and Fords were raced, and by '68, nearly all the cars were intermediates.

Below: *Petty Enterprises ran the new downsized Plymouths in 1962, accounting for the bulk of the make's 11 victories.*

Above: *Odds were good in 1961 that a Pontiac (#8 shown here on the pole) would win any given race, yet Chevrolet (on the outside and at right) took the Manufacturers' Championship. The following year, Pontiac again won the most races, but this time, the championship as well.*

1963-1965

Although the 1957 AMA ban on factory-backed racing had long been violated by manufacturers via under-the-table support for private teams, Ford came out of the closet in 1963 and waged an all-out war on the NASCAR tracks. The strategy proved effective as the company's cars won 23 of 55 events and the Manufacturers' Championship. Plymouth also made a resurgence, picking up 19 victories that year. In 1964, Ford took 30 of 62 races and another championship, but the famous Chrysler Hemi returned in Dodges and Plymouths, with the two makes combining for 26 wins. When the Hemi—and any

car fitted with it—was banned for 1965, Dodge and Plymouth pulled out of NASCAR racing in protest, allowing Ford to win a resounding 48 of 55 races and its third championship in a row.

Above: A Plymouth (left) and a Ford (right) make up the front row in this 1963 race. The two makes dominated throughout the season, with Ford garnering the most wins and the Manufacturers' Championship. The scenario was repeated for '64, despite the fact that Dodges and Plymouths were fitted with Hemi V-8s. When the Hemi was banned for '65, the Chrysler camp pulled out of NASCAR in protest, and most races concluded with a string of Fords filling the top several positions (right).

Above: *One of the few bright spots for GM during this period was at the 1963 Daytona events, where Johnny Rutherford entered his first stock car race driving a Chevrolet. He won his 100-mile qualifying event, making him the last driver to win in his NASCAR Sprint Cup Series debut.*

From the mid-'50s through 1964, most cars displayed horsepower ratings on their hoods. Starting in '65, they carried the engine's cubic-inch displacement.

1966

NASCAR rescinded its Hemi ban for 1966, and that put Plymouths **(right)** back onto the tracks—and into Victory Lane. Dodge returned as well and sweetened the pot with the fastback Charger **(far right)**, whose superior aerodynamics helped give it the most wins.

When fans didn't go for an all-Ford field, NASCAR had to let Chrysler's Hemi return for 1966. With that, Dodge and Plymouth went on a tear, winning 18 and 16 races, respectively. Ford still managed 10 victories—and won the Manufacturers' Championship—while Mercury had two, but the real surprise was that some Chevys were once again competitive, with three taking the checkered flag. Perhaps because NASCAR wanted to help level the playing field, a Ford with obvious body modifications to improve aerodynamics was allowed to compete in the Dixie 400. It was leading the race but then crashed, so no complaints were filed.

"I ain't never seen anybody who could drive a banana at 150 mile 'n hour."
—Anonymous

Left: With the return of the Hemi-engined Chryslers, Ford suddenly found itself outgunned. To help even the odds, NASCAR allowed an obviously modified Ford with a chopped roof, sloped nose, and raised tail to compete. Jokingly referred to as "The Yellow Banana," it crashed while leading the race.

1967

Once again, Hemi-equipped cars cleaned house, but this time, Plymouth netted 31 wins to just five for Dodge—largely because Richard Petty, who won an astounding 27 races that year, drove a Plymouth. Yet Ford managed to win the Manufacturers' Championship with 10 victories, while Chevy earned three. Probably because a highly-modified Ford had been allowed to race in '66, famed "inventive" mechanic Smokey Yunick entered the Daytona 500 with a Chevy Chevelle that was narrowed and shortened to about ⅞ scale. It took the pole but blew its engine during the race. After that, NASCAR began checking cars with body templates.

Above: *A Ford on the inside and Richard Petty's Plymouth on the outside battle for position at Martinsville in 1967. Plymouth won the most races, but Ford won the championship.* **Right:** *Inexplicably, the sleek Dodge Chargers dropped from 18 wins in '66 to just five in '67.*

Starting in 1967, NASCAR rules were changed to allow teams to reinforce or alter frames in the interest of safety. This mostly affected Dodges and Plymouths, which were of unibody design, as it allowed them to run specially built frames as long as the stock body dimensions were kept.

Far left: *Known for his imaginative interpretation of the rules, mechanic Smokey Yunick got a roughly ⅞-scale Chevy Chevelle through tech inspection. With its narrowed body providing less wind resistance, it became the first car to qualify at Daytona at more than 180 mph. Shortly thereafter, NASCAR began using body templates* **(left)** *to determine proper dimensions.*

1968

Torino WINS Rebel 400

Torino—
Success Car '68
The record speaks for itself

Big Savings now at your Ford Dealer's SEE-THE-LIGHT Sale!

Top row: *Both Ford and Plymouth referred to their NASCAR connections in print ads.*

The Missing Link.

Ford introduced a midsize Torino fast-back for 1968 that proved to have superior aerodynamics on NASCAR's faster tracks. The Mercury Montego sported a similar profile. The slippery design helped Ford win 21 races and the championship, while Mercury won six. But Dodge and Plymouth entries also boasted sleek new bodies, keeping them in the hunt with five and 16 victories, respectively.

Left: *Dodge had a redesigned Charger for 1968 (outside of front row), but it didn't do any better in NASCAR competition than the previous version. Both the newly introduced Ford Torino (inside of front row) and its sibling Mercury Montego (outside of second row) did better.*

1969

Chrysler Corporation and Ford Motor Company waged an aero war for 1969 that took "slippery" to new heights. NASCAR rules stated that only 500 copies of a car had to be made available for retail sale in order to qualify as "production," so Ford built a special Torino with a slanted snout, called it the Talladega, and put it on the track. Mercury offered a similar car as the Cyclone Spoiler. Dodge countered with one of the most radical speedway warriors NASCAR fans had ever seen: a Charger with a needle nose and tall rear wing called the Daytona. Ford won more races and its seventh championship in a row, but once they appeared midway through the season, Daytonas were tough to beat on the high-speed tracks.

Mercury's version of the Torino Talladega was called the Cyclone Spoiler, and it likewise enjoyed a fair degree of success on the track.

Above: *Ford started 1969's aero war with a sloped-snout Torino called the Talladega. Dodge fought back mid-season with the needle-nosed, high-winged Daytona* **(left)**. *Both could be found in street dress at the dealer nearest you, though in very limited quantities.*

The two-year-old machinery campaigned by some drivers looked like the boxes the new cars came in. Here, a 1967 Plymouth huffs its way around Daytona in 1969.

1970

Bottom left: *Ford's Torino was redesigned for 1970, but the new shape didn't fare well in testing, so the '69 Talladegas returned for another year. Overall, they weren't up to the combined assault of the new Plymouth Superbird and carry-over Dodge Daytona, now in its first full season of competition.*

Left: *Plymouth got its own winged warrior for 1970 in the form of the Road Runner-based Superbird. The similar Dodge Daytona (bottom right) wasn't carried over for 1970, but several drivers raced—and won—in year-old versions.*

Plymouth joined its sleek Dodge Daytona cousin with the pointy-beak, high-winged Superbird for 1970, which made its mark by winning 21 of 48 races. Dodge no longer offered the Daytona for 1970, but the year-old cars were still allowed to run. They racked up another 17 victories and took the Manufacturers' Championship, giving 38 of 48 to Chrysler Corp. Ford introduced a new Torino for 1970, but it proved slower than the Talladega, so the Ford and Mercury teams ran year-old equipment as well, splitting 10 wins between them.

In order to curb ever-increasing speeds—and driver concerns—NASCAR mandated restrictor plates midway through the 1970 season. The plate had four holes cut in it (one for each barrel of a four-barrel carburetor) and was placed between the carburetor and intake manifold. These holes were smaller than the barrels had been and thus restricted the air/fuel charge being fed to the cylinders. A secondary effect was that the playing field was leveled because NASCAR dictated different size holes for different engines. The plate's effectiveness is evidenced by the qualifying speeds at Talladega, the circuit's fastest track. In 1970, the pole winner qualified at 199.658 mph; in '71, the top qualifier ran 185.869 mph.

1971

The last "winged" Chrysler Corp. car to run a NASCAR Sprint Cup Series race finished seventh in the Daytona 500 despite being saddled with a smaller mandated engine. Other than that, all the Dodge and Plymouth teams fielded 1971-model cars during the '71 season. At the end of the year, Plymouth had netted 22 wins and the Manufacturers' Championship, while Mercury made a surprisingly strong showing with 12 victories, followed by Dodge with seven and Ford with four. In another surprise, Chevrolet returned to the NASCAR circuit and managed three wins.

Left: *Plymouths were redesigned for 1971 along the lines of their Dodge Charger siblings and won the most races along with the Manufacturers' Championship.* **Bottom:** *Chevrolet made an unexpected return to NASCAR and scored an equally unexpected three victories. The model used was the Monte Carlo, introduced the year before.*

Right: *NASCAR enacted new engine-size limits in 1971 to reduce speeds. While other cars could use 366-cid engines or "restricted" engines up to 430 cid, the winged Chryslers were limited to just 305 cid. One so equipped (bottom car) finished seventh in the Daytona 500. It proved to be the final NASCAR Sprint Cup Series appearance for Chrysler's winged wonders. At top is a redesigned 1971 Dodge Charger running a restricted 426 Hemi.* **Right:** *The Mercury Montego received a facelift for 1971 and fared tremendously well in NASCAR competition, netting Mercury a second-place finish in the championship race.*

New rules went into effect for 1971 to deal with the ever-increasing speeds on the faster tracks. Teams could use a "restricted" engine of up to 430 cubic inches, or they could run an unrestricted engine of up to 366 cubic inches.

1972

Detroit's "Big Three" were almost equally represented in the win column in 1972, as Chevrolet took 10 victories and the Manufacturers' Championship, Mercury racked up nine with a restyled Montego, Plymouth had eight, and Dodge four. Surprisingly, Ford garnered zero. In another surprise, American Motors Corp., last represented in NASCAR by Hudson in the mid-1950s, returned in a full factory effort with the company's midsize Matador. The cars didn't score any wins but were at least competitive.

Top right: *Amazingly, Chevrolet went from spectator to a Manufacturers' Championship in two years.* **Below:** *Plymouth went the other way, dropping from first to fourth in manufacturers' points in one year.*

Left: *A redesigned Montego brought Mercury nine wins and a runner-up finish in the Manufacturers' Championship. At least according to the hood decals, most teams chose to continue using a big-block engine fitted with a restrictor plate rather than the 366-cid unrestricted alternative. Not so for the American Motors Matador, however* **(left),** *a new entry into NASCAR. It marked the first time since the mid-'50s Hudsons that AMC actively campaigned in NASCAR Sprint Cup Series competition.*

1973-1974

Mercury won the victory battle but not the championship war in 1973.

Mercury reigned supreme in the victory column for '73, winning 11 times in a year that featured only 28 races. Dodge took eight, Chevrolet seven. Plymouth scored one victory, as did the AMC Matador. In 1974, Chevy was the big winner with 12 victories, followed by Dodge with 10, Mercury with seven, and AMC with one. Chevrolet won the Manufacturers' Championship in both years, and Ford didn't manage a win in either year.

Left: *A redesigned Chevrolet Chevelle (top car) entered NASCAR competition in 1973. The Chevy Monte Carlo was also redesigned, but most teams stuck with the earlier version (middle car). Returning with few changes was the Dodge Charger (bottom car).*

Right: *"New" Chevy Chevelles (top car) battled "old" Chevy Monte Carlos for the last time in 1974.* **Bottom left:** *American Motors redesigned its Matador for 1974 and again competed in NASCAR with a full factory effort. As in '73, the team scored one win on the season.* **Far right:** *A surprising number of different models were represented in NASCAR during 1974. Leading this pack is a Mercury Montego, followed by a Dodge Charger, an "old" Ford Torino, and an AMC Matador. And, of course, Chevy fielded two models, the Chevelle and Monte Carlo.*

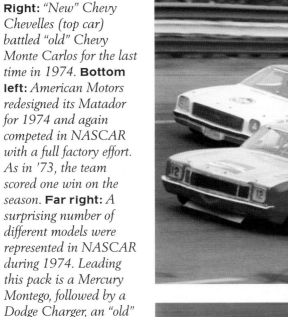

1975-1976

In the 1975 Manufacturers' Championship race, Dodge ended up ahead of Chevrolet—just as in this photo.

Left: *After a lengthy dry spell, Ford roared back with four wins in 1975.* **Below:** *AMC nearly matched that with three wins, but after '75, the company pulled out.*

Five makes scored victories in 1975: Chevrolet, Dodge, Ford, Mercury, and AMC. Dodge took 14—and the Manufacturers' Championship—followed by Chevy with six and Ford with four; Mercury and AMC took three each. Chevrolet was top banana and took the championship in '76 with 13 wins to Mercury's 10, Dodge's six, and Ford's one.

NASCAR made yet another engine-rule change for 1975, but this one would stick for a while. The displacement limit was set at 358 cubic inches—period. Because all engines were now essentially the same size and the displacement didn't match those of production engines, cars no longer trumpeted the engine's cubic inches on their hoods.

Right: *Chevrolet turned the tables on Dodge and took the 1976 championship.* **Far right:** *Mercury tipped the table even further that year, taking second in the championship race and relegating Dodge to third.*

1977-1978

Left: *The Dodge Charger was making its final appearance in this form in 1977, having been redesigned with a boxier profile for '76 that proved to be an aerodynamic nightmare. Dodge's seven victories would be its last until the 2000s.*

Above: *A pair of second-generation Monte Carlos—which actually debuted in showrooms in 1973—trails a sibling Chevelle.*

During the 1977 and '78 NASCAR seasons, GM scored by far the most wins, but although Chevy took the Manufacturers' Championship both years, not all the victories were scored by the Chevrolet nameplate. Chevy took 21 of 30 events in '77—the only other makes to score victories being Dodge with seven and Mercury with two—but the following year, Oldsmobile returned to the NASCAR fray and won a season-high 12 races, marking the first time an Olds had taken the checkered flag since 1959. Chevy scored nine victories, Ford fought back with five wins, and Mercury took four.

Above: *The strong Chevy showing in 1977 left Mercury with only two wins that year.* **Left:** *Oldsmobile returned with a vengeance in 1978, racking up 12 wins—the make's first since 1959. The #11 car was driven by Cale Yarborough, who won the NASCAR Sprint Cup Series championship.*

1979-1980

Chevrolet came roaring back for 1979 and 1980 with 19 wins the first year, 21 the second, and the Manufacturers' Championship for both. Ford amassed eight over the two seasons, as did Oldsmobile, with Mercury accounting for six.

Torinos, which hadn't been offered in showrooms since 1976, were making their final NASCAR appearances in 1979–80.

The "Colonnade" Olds Cutlass, which hadn't been built since 1977, also made its last run in 1980. A restyled version of the Cutlass would briefly take its place.

Some Ford and Mercury teams still fielded big '70s-era cars in 1980, even though production models were downsized for that year. Shown is Bobby Allison's Mercury Montego, which was similar to the Ford Thunderbird.

Above: *Although Chevrolet had gone to a smaller, trimmer Monte Carlo for the 1978 model year, NASCAR teams still raced the larger 1973–77-era versions through 1980.* **Left:** *A Mercury Montego—shown leading—won for the final time in 1980. Note how all the cars ran with their stock-looking five-mph bumpers.*

In what would later prove a pivotal rule change, teams were allowed to fabricate their own frames according to NASCAR specs starting in 1980. Safety and standardization were likely the original reasons, but down the road, it would allow front-wheel-drive bodies to be mounted on rear-wheel-drive chassis.

1981-1982

It was a surprising couple of seasons as Buick—a nameplate that hadn't won a NASCAR event since 1955—burst onto the NASCAR Sprint Cup Series scene with 22 wins in 1981 followed by 25 in '82 and the Manufacturers' Championship in both years. By contrast, Oldsmobile and Mercury flamed out, neither make scoring a victory during the period. Ford took nine races over the two seasons, Chevrolet four. In another surprise, a Pontiac won a race in 1981, the make's first checkered flag since 1963.

Right: *The downsized Thunderbirds that appeared in showrooms for 1980 became Ford's NASCAR entry in '81.*

Above: *In 1981, Buick (shown in foreground) re-entered the NASCAR fray in a big way, winning the Manufacturers' Championship two years straight. Chevrolet teams switched to the downsized Monte Carlo (background) during the period.*

Right: *While fastback rooflines were all the rage a decade earlier, cars of the early '80s tended to sport notchback profiles.*

Left: *Shown behind a new Thunderbird is a Pontiac Grand Prix, which won one race for the make in 1981. It was the first time a Pontiac had won a NASCAR Sprint Cup Series race in nearly two decades.*

Just as Detroit's production offerings were being downsized, NASCAR reduced the standard wheelbase on NASCAR Sprint Cup Series cars from 115 inches to 110 starting with the second race of the 1981 season, the Daytona 500. At the season opener at Riverside, teams could run either size car. That race was won by a long-wheelbase Chevy Monte Carlo.

1983-1985

What started as a four-way fight in the 1983 season ended with a one-on-one battle during 1985. Chevrolet finished 1983 with 15 wins and won the championship, while Buick, Pontiac, and Ford won six, five, and four, respectively. For 1984, the numbers changed a bit but not the players, Chevy again dominating the season. In '85, neither Buick nor Pontiac reached Victory Lane, leaving Chevy and Ford to split the year's 28 races evenly between them, with Chevrolet taking the championship for the third year in a row.

Right: *Pontiac remained in the hunt in 1983 and '84 with its Grand Prix, shown here trailing a Chevy Monte Carlo.* **Below:** *By 1985, the square-cut Chevy Monte Carlo (shown) was beginning to look a bit dated compared to the rounded Ford Thunderbird, the latter of which worked its way up to tie Chevy in victories for the season.*

Above: *The sporty Monte Carlo SS introduced for 1983 wore a slippery new nose, which quickly made its way into the NASCAR arena. It helped Chevy take the Manufacturers' Championship three years running.* **Left and below:** *Ford replaced its boxy Thunderbird with a much sleeker design for 1983, and it quickly became the company's mainstay in NASCAR competition.*

1986–1987

For the first time in more than a decade—and in a complete turnaround from 1985's two-make contest—five nameplates reached Victory Lane during the 1986 season. Chevrolet was again the big winner, taking 19 of 29 contests and the championship, but the rest were split among Buick, Ford, Oldsmobile, and Pontiac. All but Olds won again in '87, when Chevy topped Ford 15 wins to 11 for another championship.

Left: *For 1986, both Oldsmobile (#55 shown at back right) and Buick fielded what in production form were front-wheel-drive full-size models that were mounted on rear-wheel-drive chassis for racing. Meanwhile, Pontiac built a production version of its Grand Prix with a slanted rear window and modified nose (#27 in foreground) that aided aerodynamics.*

Right: *Similar to the Grand Prix, Chevy offered a "glassback" Monte Carlo SS Aero Coupe in 1986 and ran the more aerodynamic design in NASCAR competition.*

Left: *The fastest car ever to qualify for a NASCAR race was Bill Elliott's 1987 Thunderbird that circled Talladega at more than 212 mph. Note its smoother front end compared to that of the 1986 #15 T-Bird in the top photo.*

In one of the most radical departures from being "stock" cars, both Buick and Oldsmobile fielded entries in 1986 that in production form were redesigned full-size front-wheel-drive models, but had somewhat altered bodies mounted on rear-wheel-drive chassis for NASCAR racing. When GM moved its mid-size models to front-drive platforms in 1987, versions of these cars were likewise fitted to rear-drive racing chassis for NASCAR competition. It was also during this period that race cars began adopting smoother, more aerodynamic front ends featuring prominent spoilers. Not coincidentally, qualifying speeds hit a new high, prompting NASCAR officials to bring back carburetor restrictor plates for events run at Daytona and Talladega, the two fastest tracks on the circuit. That mandate remains in effect to this day.

1988-1989

Diversity was again the name of the game in 1988 as Ford garnered nine victories while Chevy and a surging Pontiac both took eight wins and Olds and Buick each took two. Chevrolet beat out Ford 13 to eight in '89, when Pontiac won six races and Olds and Buick each won once. Chevrolet won the Manufacturers' Championship both years. Aerodynamics were being stressed to the point that headlights were often flush not only with the fenders but also with minimized grilles, leaving a featureless face that was sometimes difficult to identify.

Right: *A redesigned Olds Cutlass that was front-wheel drive in production form but rear-drive in racing trim leads a pair of Monte Carlos, which were rear-wheel drive in production form.*
Bottom left: *The Chevrolet Monte Carlo (bottom car) and Ford Thunderbird (top car) were now the only two NASCAR competitors that started life as rear-drive models. Thunderbirds got a redesign for 1989 (shown) that gave them slightly more aerodynamic contours. Chevrolet replaced the Monte Carlo in mid-1989 with the Lumina, a front-drive car in production form.*

Above: *Bill Elliott's Thunderbird returned for 1988 but all its power didn't, at least for the high-speed Daytona and Talladega tracks, where NASCAR now mandated the use of restrictor plates.* **Left:** *Buick raced a front-wheel-drive Regal mounted on a rear-drive chassis, and Pontiac did the same with a new Grand Prix* **(bottom right.)**

1990-1992

Chevrolet barely edged out Ford 13 wins to 11 in 1990, with Pontiac taking three, Olds one, and Buick one. It would prove to be the last NASCAR Sprint Cup Series win for a Buick. The competition got tighter in '91, as Chevy won 11 races to Ford's 10, while Olds was in the hunt with five and Pontiac had three. Ford ended up atop the win column in '92 with 16 victories, leaving Chevy with eight, Pontiac with three, and Olds with its final two wins in NASCAR Sprint Cup Series competition. Chevrolet won the championship in '90 and '91, while Ford ended Chevy's nine-year streak by taking the championship in '92.

Top left: *In 1990, the Lumina took the Manufacturers' Championship in its first full year carrying the Chevrolet banner.* **Above:** *A Thunderbird—now the only NASCAR competitor that started life in rear-drive form—sits outside the draft created by a Pontiac Grand Prix and Buick Regal.*

Right: *It was a Cutlass that earned Oldsmobile its last NASCAR victory in 1992.* **Far right:** *Although better known for racing Plymouths, Richard Petty piloted a Pontiac Grand Prix in his final NASCAR appearance in 1992.*

Right and far right: *Due to a quest for better aerodynamics that led to bodies no longer appearing "stock," it was beginning to get difficult to tell one make from another without looking at the hood decal.*

1993-1996

It was a three-way battle in 1993, and the outcome couldn't have been much closer. Surprisingly, Pontiac topped the win list with 11 victories followed by Ford with 10 and Chevrolet with nine. Chevrolet took the championship. For '94, it was a Ford-Chevy shootout, Ford coming out on top with 20 wins and the championship to Chevy's 11. The tables were turned for '95, Chevy taking 21 victories and the championship to Ford's eight, with Pontiac bouncing back for two. It was a Chevy repeat in '96 with 17 wins and the championship to Ford's 13 victories, while Pontiac garnered one. During this period, many cars had headlights that were mere outlines mimicking production-car features on an otherwise "aero-formed" nose.

Top: *Pontiac's Grand Prix pulled off an upset in 1993 by winning the most races, though not the Manufacturers' Championship for Pontiac.* **Above:** *Chevy and Ford battled it out for the 1993 championship, with Chevy taking the trophy.* **Right:** *Chevy and Ford were at it again in 1994, but this time, Ford came out on top.* **Bottom:** *Thunderbirds continued to represent Ford in NASCAR Sprint Cup Series competition during the 1993–96 time frame, but would not for much longer.*

Left: *The three makes competing in NASCAR Sprint Cup Series competition in 1995 were Pontiac (leading), Chevrolet (left), and Ford (right). Chevrolet switched from Luminas to Monte Carlos that year.* **Bottom:** *A 1996 Monte Carlo shows off its tape-stripe "headlights."*

1997-1999

Ford won 19 races and the Manufacturers' Championship in 1997 versus 11 for Chevrolet and two for Pontiac. Chevy edged out Ford in both wins and the championship in '98 with 16 victories to Ford's 15, while Pontiac again scored two. Ford followed GM's mid-'80s lead in 1998 and replaced its Thunderbird bodyshells with ones mimicking that of a Taurus—which was a front-wheel-drive four-door sedan. For 1999, Ford recaptured the "most wins" category and the championship with 13 to Chevy's 12, but Pontiac made an impressive showing with nine victories. It was during this time that cars began sporting headlight decals to make them look more like their showroom counterparts.

Right: *Ford replaced the Thunderbird with the Taurus for 1998 (right two cars), which in showrooms was a front-drive four-door sedan. Note that the Tauruses, along with the Monte Carlo (black car) and Pontiac Grand Prix (green car) had headlight decals.* **Below:** *All cars now sported similar profiles.*

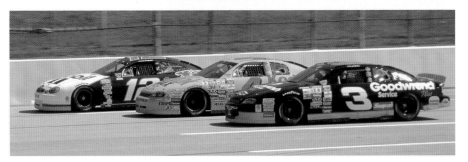

Above: *The Ford Thunderbird was discontinued after 1997, making that the last year the model represented Ford in NASCAR competition (bottom two cars). During the '97 season, Chevy Monte Carlos (top car) adopted headlight decals in place of mere outlines to give them a more recognizable "face."* **Left:** *Thanks to distinct grilles, headlight decals, and prominent name badges, the three makes competing in NASCAR could be easily identified—at least from the front.*

2000-2002

Above: *A pointier snout graces this 2000 Taurus. The car took home that year's Manufacturers' Championship for Ford.*

ord led in wins for 2000 with 14 and took the Manufacturers' Championship, but second place went—surprisingly—to Pontiac, which took 11 victories to Chevrolet's nine. The big news for 2001 was not that Chevy rebounded to nail the championship with 16 trips to Victory Lane, but that Dodge returned to Victory Lane for the first time since 1977. The company

made a full-fledged effort with its redesigned Intrepid and was rewarded with four checkered flags. Meanwhile, Ford took 11 races while Pontiac took five. Dodge made an even better showing in 2002 with seven wins, though Ford was back on top with 14 and the championship, followed by Chevy with 10. Pontiac trailed with five victories.

Above, center: *Monte Carlos again represented Chevrolet in 2000, but not as successfully as in the past.* **Above:** *In 2000, Pontiac enjoyed its best season since 1993, coming in second behind Ford with 11 wins.*

Above, left to right: *Dodge returned to NASCAR in 2001 with a car based on its front-drive Intrepid. Chevrolet nosed out Ford for the 2001 championship. Pontiac continued in 2001 with its Grand Prix.*

Far left: *Ford took the championship back from Chevrolet in 2002.* **Left:** *Dodge had an impressive sophomore season in 2002, netting seven wins and beating out Pontiac for third in the championship race.*

2003-2006

Above: *Chevrolet won the Manufacturers' Championship in 2003, but surprisingly, Dodge beat out Ford for second place.*

Pontiac scored only one win in 2003, which would turn out to be its last; the company withdrew from NASCAR after the end of the season, and GM has since killed the Pontiac nameplate. Chevrolet won the Manufacturers' Championship that year, as it would through

2013. In 2005, both Dodge and Ford switched models for NASCAR competition; Dodge replaced the Intrepid with the Charger, which in production form was a rear-wheel-drive sedan, while Ford went from the Taurus to its new mid-size front-wheel-drive car, the Fusion.

Above: *For 2004, Dodge's NASCAR entry (leading car) wore a slightly revised face, while Ford campaigned the Taurus (trailing car) for the last time.* **Below, center:** *Chevrolet continued to be represented by the Monte Carlo in 2004, which brought the company the championship.* **Below:** *Starting in 2005, Ford switched to the Fusion (leading car) while Dodge based its offering on its new Charger rear-drive sedan.*

Right: *Pontiac's Grand Prix (right) suffered a tough year in 2003, which would turn out to be its last season in NASCAR Sprint Cup Series competition.*

Right: *Chevrolet won its third straight championship in 2006 with the Monte Carlo, which that year adopted the "SS" suffix to reflect a new production offering equipped with a V-8 engine.*

2007

NASCAR's long-awaited new car design, which had been in development for seven years, debuted in select races during 2007. Four inches higher and two inches wider than its predecessor, it was designed to improve safety, decrease costs, and increase competition by limiting speeds. Also that year, Toyota joined the NASCAR fray with the Camry—actually two Camrys, as one was of the "old" design while the other followed the new formula. Chevrolet continued its streak of Manufacturers' Championships, winning its fifth in a row.

Below: *Toyota entered NASCAR Sprint Cup Series competition in 2007 with a car bearing the "Camry" nameplate.*

Left and below: *A new car design was phased in during 2007, so teams ran both the "old" cars (left) and the new version (below) that year. The new car was not only taller and wider than before, but also had a more blunt nose with a large, underhanging splitter along with a separate rear wing.*

2008-2009

Although the original plan was to run the new car design in 26 of 36 races in 2008, the decision was made to use it in all events that year. Toyota won its first NASCAR race in its 40th attempt, marking the first time a foreign nameplate had won in NASCAR Sprint Cup Series competition since a Jaguar took the checkered flag at a road-race course in 1954. Chevrolet once again won the Manufacturers' Championship, locking up its sixth win in a row. The company made it seven in a row in 2009.

2010-2012

The Gen-5 car introduced during the 2007 season continued to evolve as the teams and NASCAR learned more about it. During 2010, the rear wing was replaced with a spoiler, and in 2011, the noses of the cars were reconfigured to a more streamlined and conventional configuration. The following year, fuel injection replaced carburetors on all NASCAR Sprint Cup Series cars. Chevrolet continued its dominance by taking the manufacturers title for the 2010, 2011, and 2012 seasons. This gave Chevrolet 10 consecutive Manufacturers' Championships.

Left: *Jimmie Johnson in the #48 Chevrolet and Kurt Busch in the #2 Miller Lite Dodge run wheel-to-wheel in the 2010 Food City 500 at Bristol in March. This was the last race in which cars used a rear wing. Thereafter, they were fitted with a conventional spoiler that generated an additional 100 lbs. of downforce, as shown on Clint Bowyer's #33 Chevrolet* (Right). *Note that the noses of these cars still carried the pavement-scraping splitter with external braces, an aero element that was in its final season. Note also the "shark fin" on the left side of the rear window designed to increase side force.*

Left: *Matt Kenseth's #17 Ford displays the new streamlined nose introduced for 2011.*
Below left: *For 2012, all cars running in the NASCAR Sprint Cup Series switched from carburetors to fuel injection. NASCAR said the change would "provide greater fuel efficiency and a greener footprint, while maintaining the same great competition."* **Below right:** *After returning to the NASCAR Sprint Cup Series in 2001, Dodge withdrew at the end of the 2012 season. Brad Keselowski in the #2 Dodge scored the manufacturer's last win at the September 30th AAA400.*

2013—

In 2013, cars competing in the NASCAR Sprint Cup Series wore all-new bodies with more "personality." Designed with car manufacturers, they looked more like the street versions of the Chevrolet SS, Ford Fusion, and Toyota Camry. Chevrolet continued its dominance of the series, winning its 11th and 12th consecutive Manufacturers' Championships in 2013 and 2014.

The Gen-6 cars that debuted for 2013 were fitted with completely new bodies; they replaced the Gen-5 cars that had been introduced during the 2007 season. The hood and deck lid were made of lightweight carbon fiber, and the bodylines more closely resembled the street versions of the respective cars to give brand identity. The cars were also 160 lbs. lighter, despite having several new bars added to the rollcage structure to improve roof integrity. In addition to the new bodies, NASCAR allowed teams to put the driver's name at the top of the windshield, along with a sponsor name at the back of the roof. With the departure of Dodge after the 2012 season, the three competing makes in the NASCAR Sprint Cup Series were the Ford Fusion **(Above)***, Chevrolet SS* **(Below left)***, and Toyota Camry* **(Below right)***.*

CHAPTER THREE

THE TRACKS

In NASCAR's early years, most of the racing venues were flat dirt ovals of less than one mile in length, sometimes referred to as "bullrings." Exceptions included the famed Daytona Beach & Road Course, a 4.15-mile elongated oval utilizing a stretch of Daytona Beach linked to a section of adjoining Highway A1A; and Darlington Raceway, a paved, banked, 1.366-mile egg-shaped oval that earned distinction as NASCAR's first superspeedway. Eventually, paved tracks became the norm, with the last dirt-track race being held in 1970. If the drivers and cars are modern gladiators and chariots, these tracks are their Coliseum.

Although a few road courses have long dotted the NASCAR schedule, most of today's tracks are roughly oval in shape; many have a curved frontstretch, and these are referred to as "tri-ovals." Shown is Daytona International Speedway, first and perhaps best-known of the tri-oval superspeedways.

Daytona Beach & Road Course

As its name implied, the Daytona Beach & Road Course combined a stretch of beach with a section of adjacent Highway A1A to form one of NASCAR's earliest and most notable venues. The hard-packed sands of Daytona Beach had been used for speed-record runs since the early 1900s, and in the mid '30s, a strip of beach was joined with A1A to create a race track. Originally 3.2 miles in length, the elongated oval was expanded to 4.15 miles in the late 1940s, resulting in two-mile straightaways. The tight, sandy turns that connected them often became deeply rutted during the course of a race, which was tough on cars and drivers alike and caused numerous accidents and rollovers. The first race was for 40 laps or 166 miles, but the following year's contest was lengthened to 48 laps/200 miles. When only half the cars managed to finish, it was cut down to 39 laps/160 miles, where it remained through its last race in 1958. A restaurant now stands at 4511 South Atlantic Avenue, the site of the famous race track's north turn.

Above: *Even cars of the early '50s could build up tremendous speed on Daytona's two-mile straightaways that then had to be scrubbed off to negotiate the tight, sandy corners.* **Right:** *A shot of the track's north turn reveals the deep ruts that would be carved into the sandy corners during a race.*

Left: *Today, an outdoor patio that's part of the Racing's North Turn Bar & Grille overlooks the track's famous north turn.*

North Wilkesboro Speedway

Right and far right: *North Wilkesboro is the kind of classic oval short track that was a common venue in NASCAR's early years. With its original dirt racing surface, it was among the many "bullrings" on the annual schedule.* **Far middle right:** *After being paved in 1957, it continued hosting NASCAR events until 1996, by which time it had become somewhat antiquated compared with the newer tracks.* **Far bottom right:** *Still standing but in need of attention, North Wilkesboro reopened in 2010 for three non-NASCAR races, but closed again the following year.*

One of the more famous early NASCAR short-track venues was the .625-mile North Wilkesboro Speedway located about four miles east of North Wilkesboro, North Carolina. The track opened in 1947, hosted its first NASCAR Strictly Stock race in '49, and had two race dates a year starting in 1951. Originally a dirt oval, the track was paved midway through the 1957 season with 14-degree turns. An unusual feature of the track is that the frontstretch runs slightly downhill while the backstretch runs uphill. The last NASCAR Sprint Cup Series event held there was in 1996, after which the track's two race dates were moved to New Hampshire Motor Speedway and Texas Motor Speedway. Thereafter, relatively few races were held at North Wilkesboro, and the track fell into disrepair.

Lakewood Speedway

Over the years, the one-mile Lakewood Speedway played host to horse, motorcycle, and automobile races, and the infield lake was used for boat races.

Located south of Atlanta in Lakewood, Georgia, Lakewood Speedway opened in 1919 adjacent to the Lakewood Fairgrounds. NASCAR events were held on the one-mile dirt oval starting in 1951 and continued through 1959. After that, NASCAR moved the race to the newly opened Atlanta International Raceway, a 1.5-mile paved superspeedway that is today known as Atlanta Motor Speedway. Lakewood continued in operation until the late 1970s. Today, much of the site is covered by a parking lot and a couple of roads.

Much of the "infield grass" at Lakewood was actually water, and it wasn't unheard-of for out-of-control drivers to end up in the drink.

Raleigh Speedway

Originally called Southland Speedway when it opened in the early 1950s, the name had been changed to Raleigh Speedway by the time the first NASCAR race was hosted there in 1953. Paved and measuring one mile in length, it was a fast track for its day and one of the first to boast lighting for nighttime racing. The last NASCAR race was run at Raleigh in 1958, and the track closed shortly thereafter. It was torn down in 1967 and eventually replaced by an industrial park.

Located near Raleigh, North Carolina, Raleigh Speedway was an elongated oval with lengthy straightaways and tight, 16-degree-banked corners. The infield held a ¼-mile track used for NASCAR Modified and NASCAR Sportsman races.

NASCAR races at Raleigh Speedway were typically 100 to 300 miles in length. From 1956 through 1958, the races were held on the fourth of July.

Martinsville Speedway

Right and far right: *Martinsville started out as a half-mile dirt oval with tight turns at each end. NASCAR races have been held there since the organization's inaugural 1948 season.*

Known as "The Paperclip" for its elongated shape, Martinsville Speedway is the oldest track still hosting NASCAR races. In operation since the late 1940s, it's also the shortest, and poses a challenge to brakes as the cars must slow dramatically to negotiate its tight, low-banked turns. In Martinsville's long history, it has hosted such famous races as the Virginia 500 (1959–1981 and 2001–2003), the Old Dominion 500 (1960–1982 and 2001–2002), and in 2013, the STP Gas Booster 500 and the Goody's Headache Relief Shot 500. These "500" races are for 500 laps.

> "Martinsville is not an anger management seminar. In fact, it might do you some good to attend one of those before the race."
>
> —Kevin Lepage

Left: *Martinsville's dirt track was paved with asphalt in the mid-1950s. It received concrete corners in the mid-70s due to wear caused by the heavy braking and turning forces required to negotiate its tight, low-banked (12-degree) corners. Races held there tend to be action-packed demo derbies resulting in lots of paint-swapping, bent sheetmetal, and caution flags. The fastest qualifying speed of 2013 was just under 100 mph.*

Langhorne Speedway

Circular Langhorne Speedway in Pennsylvania was one of the earliest NASCAR racing venues. The one-mile dirt track contained no straightaways. Drivers who tackled the fickle monster had to run flat-out for the entire distance—often in a four-wheel drift—making Langhorne one of the most punishing and dangerous racing facilities ever built. The last NASCAR race was held there in 1957, but after being paved in 1965, Langhorne hosted open-wheel races until the early '70s. The site is now home to a shopping center.

Langhorne played host to NASCAR events from the organization's beginning through 1957. A race at Langhorne was essentially a 200-mile left-hand turn, punishing on both drivers and machinery.

Left: *Today, a historical marker stands in a parking lot at the site of what was once Langhorne Speedway.*

Darlington Raceway

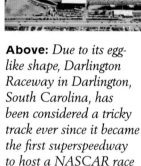

Above: *Due to its egg-like shape, Darlington Raceway in Darlington, South Carolina, has been considered a tricky track ever since it became the first superspeedway to host a NASCAR race in 1950.*

Above: *A 1.366-mile length and corners with a maximum banking of 25 degrees allowed a top qualifying speed of just under 182 mph in 2013.*

"Anybody who can win at Darlington ought to change his uniform in a phone booth and leap tall buildings in a single bound."

—Sterling Marlin

Darlington is the granddaddy of super-speedways, having opened its gates in 1950 when most NASCAR races were held on short dirt tracks. As such, it has attained something of a mythical aura among older race car drivers and fans. The big oval has a slightly egg-like shape because the original owner wanted to preserve a minnow pond that sat outside what is now turn four. The fact that the corners at each end have a different radius makes it tough to set up a car's suspension so that it handles well all around the track, and newer drivers who misjudge a turn and scrape the wall are said to have earned their "Darlington stripe." The track has long been home to the Southern 500—the first of the 500-mile races—as well as the Rebel 300/400/500 (1960–1978) and the Transouth 500 (1983–1999). In 2005, the schedule was cut back to just one race per year, which, starting in 2009, was once again called the Southern 500.

Richmond International Raceway

Originally a half-mile oval when it hosted its first NASCAR race in 1953, Richmond was turned into a ¾-mile tri-oval with 14-degree banking in 1988 (shown), its former front-stretch becoming pit road. The top qualifying speed in 2013 was 130.599 mph.

Richmond International Raceway has been known for running its events at night ever since lights were installed in the early '90s. A NASCAR track since 1953, it was originally a half-mile oval, being reconfigured in 1988 to its current .75-mile length. Races hosted during its long history include the Richmond 250/400/500 (1962–1983), the Capital City 300/400/500 (1962–1980), the Miller High Life/Genuine Draft 400 (1984–1995), and the Pontiac Excitement 400 (1988–2003). In 2013, Richmond hosted the Toyota Owners 400 and the Federated Auto Parts 400. These "400" races are for 400 laps, equating to 300 miles.

Watkins Glen International

Watkins Glen International is the "faster" of the two road courses on the NASCAR Sprint Cup Series schedule. Despite its numerous tight turns, the top 2013 qualifier posted a speed of 128.241 mph, a track record.

Known for much of its history as simply "The Glen," this road course in western New York state has played host to numerous forms of racing. It is one of only two road courses on the NASCAR schedule, but its lengthy 2.45-mile distance allows far higher lap speeds than at Sonoma Raceway, the only other NASCAR road course on the NASCAR Sprint Cup Series schedule. Though the first NASCAR race was held at The Glen in 1957, a seven-year hiatus followed before races were run in '64 and '65, after which they weren't held there again until 1986. "The Bud at the Glen" was run from 1986 through 1998, and in 2013, the track hosted the Cheez-It 355 at The Glen.

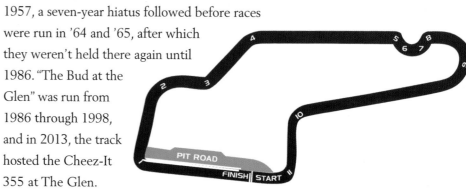

Daytona International Speedway

When it opened in 1959, the monstrous 2.5-mile Daytona track with its imposing 24-degree banking was like nothing NASCAR drivers of the day had ever seen. "There are other tracks that separated the men from the boys," said driver Jimmy Thompson. "This is the track that will separate the brave from the weak after the boys are gone."

Ask any stock car driver to pick the one race they'd most like to win, and the vast majority would probably pick the Daytona 500. Held at the Daytona International Speedway since its gates opened in 1959, the prestigious race has been run under the same name ever since and currently leads off the NASCAR season. As a steeply banked 2.5-mile tri-oval, Daytona International Speedway is second only to Talladega in length and all-time top qualifying speed. In fact, speeds at both tracks got so high (well over 200 mph in qualifying) that NASCAR has long required cars to run restrictor plates for races held there. Though the Daytona 500 is the most famous, other races hosted at the speedway over the years are the Firecracker 250/400 and Pepsi 400, with the Coke Zero 400 Powered by Coca-Cola taking the track's second race date since 2008.

Atlanta Motor Speedway

When it opened its gates to NASCAR racing in 1960, Atlanta Motor Speedway was second only to the new Daytona International Speedway in length. Atlanta is currently one of the fastest tracks on the NASCAR circuit, as the longer Daytona and Talladega tracks now require the cars to be fitted with restrictor plates that reduce top speeds. During its rich history, Atlanta has hosted such well-known races as the Dixie 300/400/500 (1960–1979), the Atlanta 500 (1960–1980), the Atlanta Journal 500 (1980–1990), the Motorcraft/Motorcraft Quality Parts 500 (1986–1994), the Coca-Cola 500 (1981–1985), and the Napa 500 (1995–2002). It now hosts just one NASCAR Sprint Cup Series race per year, which in 2013 was the AdvoCare 500.

Originally an oval, the Atlanta Motor Speedway in Hampton, Georgia, was reconfigured into a 1.54-mile tri-oval with 24-degree banking in mid-1997. A qualifying speed of just under 190 mph was reached there in 2013.

Charlotte Motor Speedway

Although the 1.5-mile Charlotte tri-oval is certainly not the longest NASCAR track or, at 24 degrees, the most steeply banked, the top qualifying speed for 2013 was 195.624 mph.

Right: *It started out as the Charlotte Motor Speedway, but the historic track in Concord, North Carolina, was renamed Lowe's Motor Speedway in 1999. Prior to the 2010 season, it reverted back to its original name.*

Originally known as Charlotte Motor Speedway, the 1.5-mile paved quad-oval in Concord, North Carolina, was the first track to be named after a corporate sponsor when it became Lowe's Motor Speedway in 1999. After the 2009 season, however, its name was changed back to Charlotte Motor Speedway. When first opened in 1960, it joined Darlington Raceway and newcomers Daytona International Speedway and Atlanta Motor Speedway (opened in 1959 and 1960, respectively) as one of the few long, paved, steeply banked superspeedways on the NASCAR circuit. The track was the first to host 600-mile races, the most prominent being the World 600 (1960–1984) and the Coca-Cola 600

(1986–present). In 2013 it played host to the Coca-Cola 600 and Bank of America 500, along with the Sprint Showdown and NASCAR Sprint All-Star Race.

Bristol Motor Speedway

Above and below: *Bristol Motor Speedway, located in hilly northeast Tennesssee, has been a NASCAR venue since 1961. It started out as a half-mile asphalt oval with 22-degree banking.*

Above: *Today, Bristol measures .533 mile and is paved in concrete. Turns that were increased to a 36-degree angle in 1969 were later given a varying pitch with a maximum probably closer to 30 degrees. In 2012, the top groove in the turns was ground down to a maximum of 28 degrees. The top qualifying speed of 2013 was 129.535 mph.*

As a half-mile oval with steep banking, drivers jokingly liken racing at Bristol to "flying jets in a gymnasium." When the cars line up for the start, they often stretch nearly halfway around the short track. As a result, Bristol is known for its "paint swapping," and races tend to include numerous accidents and caution flags. Partly due to what often seems like demo-derby action, tickets are notoriously difficult to get. Bristol was the long-time home to the Southeastern 500 and Volunteer 500 (both running from 1961 to 1979), and more recently to the Busch 500, Valleydale Meats 500, and Goody's 500. In

2013, Bristol hosted the Food City 500 and the IRWIN Tools Night Race. These "500" races are for 500 laps, which works out to 266.5 miles.

Rockingham Speedway

Often referred to as "The Rock"—a nickname that references its hosting city—Rockingham Speedway was a mainstay on the NASCAR circuit for 40 years. When it opened in 1965, it was a flat, one-mile oval but was reconfigured in 1969 as a tri-oval with fairly steep banking. Shuffling of ownership and race dates left it without a NASCAR Sprint Cup Series event after 2004, but it remains in use as a testing facility by many NASCAR teams. Over the years it played host to such races as the American 500 (1965–1981), the Carolina 500 (1967–1981), the Goodwrench 400/500 (1986–1998), and the AC Delco 400/500 (1987–1998). Closing out Rockingham's NASCAR Sprint Cup Series tenure in 2004 was the Subway 400, which had been run there since 2002.

Earlier in its history, Rockingham Speedway had been known as North Carolina Motor Speedway and North Carolina Speedway. The Rock hasn't been home to a NASCAR Sprint Cup Series event in several years, but the 1.017-mile tri-oval with 25-degree banking recently hosted NASCAR Camping World Truck Series races, and is still in use.

Dover International Speedway

Since a short track is generally defined as being less than one mile in length and a superspeedway as being more than a mile, Dover—at exactly one mile—is technically neither. Unlike most modern tracks, the racing surface is made of concrete rather than asphalt. Dover is known to be hard on cars, thus earning it the nickname "The Monster Mile." It has been the venue for such races as the Mason-Dixon 300/500 (1969–1983), the Delaware 500 (1971–1978 and 1984–1988), the Budweiser 500 (1983–1994), and several 400-milers under the MBNA banner. The 2013 schedule included the FedEx 400 benefiting Autism Speaks and the AAA 400.

Below: *The stands are packed for a 2009 race at Dover, when the top qualifying speed was 157.356 mph. Since then, the speeds have gotten faster: In 2013, the top qualifier circled the track at 161.849 mph.*

The one-mile Dover oval was originally called "Dover Downs" when it opened in 1969, and it still shares the grounds with a horse-racing track of that name; it became Dover International Speedway in 2002. Originally asphalt, the current concrete surface was poured in the mid-1990s. Turns are banked at 24 degrees.

Michigan International Speedway

The two-mile Michigan International Speedway has turns banked at only 18 degrees. Yet the fastest qualifying speeds of the 2013 NASCAR Sprint Cup Series season were run there, with some topping 200 mph.

With the longer Daytona and Talladega tracks now requiring restrictor plates on cars to reduce speeds, Michigan's long straights and wide turns make it among the fastest tracks on the current NASCAR schedule. Located in southern Michigan, the facility opened in 1968 and hosted its first NASCAR race the following year. A number of different races have been run since then, including the Yankee 600/400 (1969–1974), The Motor State 500/400 (1969–1975), the Champion Spark Plug 400 (1975–1993), and the Miller Genuine Draft 400 (1990–1995). Hosted in 2013 were the Quicken Loans 400 and the Pure Michigan 400.

Talladega Superspeedway

Talladega's monstrous 33-degree banked turns are the steepest of any superspeedway on the NASCAR schedule.

At 2.66 miles, the Talladega tri-oval became the longest superspeedway on the NASCAR schedule when it opened in 1969, and it still is. A record qualifying speed of 212.809 mph was recorded there in 1987, but due to NASCAR-mandated restrictor plates, today's qualifying speeds hover around 191 mph.

Talladega was the biggest, fastest track on the NASCAR circuit when it opened its gates in 1969 as the Alabama International Motor Speedway. In fact, many drivers thought it was *too* fast, questioning its rough racing surface and whether contemporary tires could withstand the speeds. As a result, some of the top drivers boycotted the inaugural running of the Talladega 500. Speeds at the track again became a concern in 1987 when Bill Elliott set the NASCAR record for the fastest qualifying lap at over 212 mph. The following year, NASCAR mandated that cars run restrictor plates at Talladega and Daytona to reduce speeds, and no driver has since threatened the record. Over the years, the speedway has hosted the Talladega 500 (1969–1987), the Winston 500 (1971–1993), and the Diehard 500 (1990–2000). On the 2013 schedule were the Aaron's 499 and the Camping World RV Sales 500.

The high speeds attainable on the Talladega track almost ensure the type of hair-raising action spectators witnessed at the 2003 Aaron's 499 (left), and it's not unusual to see cars airborne in the apron (below).

Pocono Raceway

Much of the Pocono track is framed by beautiful forest land.

Each of the three corners has a different radius and banking angle, making the 2.5-mile Pocono track a challenge for drivers. After being repaved in 2012, qualifying speeds jumped by more than 10 mph, with the 2013 record resting at 180.654 mph.

Pocono Raceway in eastern Pennsylvania is the only triangular track on the NASCAR Sprint Cup Series schedule. Its unique design gives it three corners, each with a different radius and banking angle, which complicates things for drivers and chassis tuners alike. Since opening its gates to NASCAR in 1974, Pocono has played host to a number of different races, including the Purolator 500 (1974–1976), the Coca-Cola 500 (1977–1980), the Miller High Life/Genuine Draft 500, the Pocono 500, and the Pennsylvania 500. In 2013, Pocono hosted the Party in the Poconos 400 and the GoBowling.com 400.

Phoenix International Raceway

Its odd shape and variable banking between 9-11 degrees in the corners limits qualifying speeds on the one-mile Phoenix track; the top qualifying speed in 2013 was 139.222 mph. Fans can enjoy not only a race, but also the surrounding desert scenery.

Commonly known as "PIR," Phoenix International Raceway opened in 1964 but didn't host a NASCAR Sprint Cup Series race until the Checker 500 in 1988. Though PIR is generally described as a tri-oval, the corners at each end of the track are of a different radius, and the backstretch contains a bend known as "the dogleg." Other races run there over the years include the Pyroil 500 (1991–1992) and the Dura Lube 500 (1995–1996). In 2013, a pair of races were on the schedule: the SUBWAY Fresh Fit 500, which has been there since 2005; and the Advocare 500. These "500" races go for 500 kilometers, or 312 miles.

Sonoma Raceway

The 1.99-mile Sonoma road course often proves a challenge to NASCAR Sprint Cup Series drivers used to turning left on banked corners. The top qualifying speed in 2013 was 94.986 mph.

Sonoma Raceway is one of only two road courses on the NASCAR circuit. Known as Sears Point Raceway before 2001 and Infineon Raceway from 2001 to 2011, the track hosted its first NASCAR race in 1989 after the closing of Riverside International Raceway, a long-time NASCAR road-racing venue. Sonoma's elevation changes and seven right-hand turns often prove challenging to stock car drivers used to racing on ovals. Since 2007, Sonoma has been home to the Toyota / SaveMart 350 and previously hosted the Banquet Frozen Foods 300 (1989–1991), the Save Mart 300 (1992), the Save Mart Supermarkets 300 (1993–1997), the Save Mart/Kragin 350 (1998–2000), and the Dodge/Save Mart 350 (2001–2006).

New Hampshire Motor Speedway

Left and far left: *The 1.058-mile New Hampshire oval has variable banking between 2-7 degrees in the corners. In 2013, the top qualifying speed was 136.497 mph.*

Sometimes referred to as "Loudon" in respect to the town in which it resides, New Hampshire Motor Speedway has hosted NASCAR Sprint Cup Series races since 1993. It started out with only one NASCAR Sprint Cup Series race a year but added a second date in 1997. Inside Loudon's oval track is a 1.6-mile road course that hosts motorcycle, sports car, and karting events. NASCAR Sprint Cup Series races that have been run on New Hampshire Motor Speedway's oval include the Slick 50 300 (1993–1995), the Jiffy Lube 300 (1996–1999), and the New Hampshire 300 (2001–2002). The New England 300 returned for 2006 after a stint in 2001–2003, and the Sylvania 300 has been run there since 2003, joined in 2013 by the Camping World RV Sales 301.

Indianapolis Motor Speedway

Above: *The 2.5-mile "rectangular oval" shape of the speedway (shown in 1930) results in 3330-foot and 3300-foot straightaways. The top qualifying speed in 2013 was 187.531 mph.*

Most famous as the site of the annual Indianapolis 500 open–wheel race that was first run in 1911, the Indianapolis Motor Speedway has long been known as "The Brickyard." (It was once paved with bricks, which are still used for "the yard of bricks" that marks the start/finish line.) In 1994, the nickname was adopted for the first NASCAR race run at Indy: the Brickyard 400. It was later called The Allstate 400 at the Brickyard and The Allstate 400. In 2013, it was the Crown Royal Presents the Samuel Deeds 400 at the Brickyard Powered by BigMachineRecords.com.

Above: *When the Indianapolis Motor Speedway first opened in 1909, it was paved with crushed stone and tar, but after a few races were held, it was repaved later that same year with more than three million bricks; it's shown here at the start of the 1931 Indy 500. Later in the 1930s, it was partially paved with tarmac, then fully paved in 1961 except for a three-foot section at the starting line. "The yard of bricks," as it became known, remains to this day.*

Texas Motor Speedway

ocated in the northeast corner of Texas in the city of Fort Worth, Texas Motor Speedway is very similar in layout to Atlanta Motor Speedway and Charlotte Motor Speedway in being a 1.5-mile quad-oval with 24-degree banking in the turns. Since opening in 1996, it has hosted a number of different NASCAR races, including the Interstate Batteries 500 (1997), the Texas 500 (1998), the Primestar 500 (1999), the DirecTV 500 (2000), the Harrah's 500 (2001), and later, the Samsung 500 and Dickies 500. Two NASCAR Sprint Cup Series events were held at Texas during 2013: the NRA 500 in April, and the AAA Texas 500 in November.

The fastest qualifier at Texas Motor Speedway in 2013 had a speed of 196.299 mph.

Auto Club Speedway

Located about 40 miles east of Los Angeles, Auto Club Speedway was originally called California Speedway when it opened its gates in 1997. Though NASCAR events use the two-mile tri-oval, the facility also features an infield road course as

Left: *Situated in the sprawling Los Angeles area, California Speedway was renamed Auto Club Speedway in early 2008.*

Right: *A pair of fighter jets flies over the two-mile tri-oval Auto Club Speedway.*

well as a drag strip, allowing the track to be used for numerous types of racing events. Past NASCAR races hosted include the NAPA Auto Parts 500, the Pop Secret 500, and the Sony HD 500. Through the 2010 season, Auto Club Speedway hosted two NASCAR Sprint Cup Series races a year, but afterward, hosted only one, and it was cut to 400 miles. For 2013, it was called the Auto Club 400.

Left: *With 14-degree banking in the turns and a 3100-foot frontstretch, the fastest qualifying speed at Auto Club Speedway in 2013 was 187.451 mph.*

Las Vegas Motor Speedway

Despite 20-degree banking, the fastest 2013 qualifier at the 1.5-mile Las Vegas tri-oval ran more than 190 mph.

ocal drag racers may run there two nights a week and the local police department might reserve it for driver training, but every March, the Las Vegas Motor Speedway reserves a day for the NASCAR Sprint Cup Series. It started in 1998 with the aptly named Las Vegas 400, then progressed to the Carsdirect.com 400, the UAW-DaimlerChrysler 400, the UAW-Dodge 400, the Shelby 427, and the Shelby American. Since 2011, Las Vegas has hosted the KOBALT Tools 400. Races feature the typical Las Vegas glitz and glitter. Among the spectacles: Lucky winners are greeted by showgirls in Victory Lane.

Jimmie Johnson enjoys the spoils of victory at Las Vegas in 2006.

Homestead-Miami Speedway

Homestead-Miami opened in 1995 as a "rectangular oval" similar in shape to the Indianapolis Motor Speedway but with much flatter corners. It was first used for CART (open-wheel) races, but the low banking was found to cut down on speeds and make passing difficult. In 1997, the track was changed to a traditional oval shape and hosted its first NASCAR Sprint Cup Series race two years later. In 2003, it was given steeper banking. Homestead-Miami has hosted the Pennzoil 400, Pennzoil Freedom 400, Ford 400, and, since 2012, the season-ending Ford EcoBoost 400.

The 1.5-mile Homestead-Miami track boasts variable banking between 18 and 20 degrees and 1760-foot straightaways. In 2013, the top qualifying speed was 177.677 mph.

Chicagoland Speedway

Located about 35 miles southwest of Chicago in Joliet, Illinois, Chicagoland Speedway is unusual in that the backstretch of this tri-oval isn't straight, but rather has a noticeable curve to it. Chicagoland hosted its first stock car race—the Tropicana 400—in July 2001. In 2011, its race date was moved to September, giving it the first event in the Chase for the NASCAR Sprint Cup. Since then, that race has been the GEICO 400.

Chicagoland Speedway is a 1.5-mile tri-oval with 18-degree banking and a 2400-foot frontstretch. The top qualifying speed in 2013 was 189.414 mph.

Kansas Speedway

Right: *The 1.5-mile Kansas Speedway was repaved and reconfigured with 17-20 variable-degree banking in 2012, resulting in faster lap times. As a result, qualifying speeds jumped by about 15 mph, reaching 191.864 in 2013.*

Bottom: *When the Banquet 400 was run at Kansas in 2003–2006, the promotional logo on the infield grass was nearly the size of a football field.*

Kansas Speedway opened its gates in June 2001 and hosted its first NASCAR Sprint Cup Series race less than four months later. In 2011, lights were added for night racing, and the track gained a second NASCAR Sprint Cup Series event. The following year, the track was repaved and reconfigured, adding variable banking in the turns. During its history, Kansas Speedway has been home to the Protection One 400, the Banquet 400 presented by ConAgra Foods, the Camping World RV 400, the LifeLock 400, and the Price Chopper 400 presented by Kraft Foods. In 2013, Kansas hosted the STP 400 in April, and the Hollywood Casino 400 in October.

Kentucky Speedway

Kentucky Speedway in Sparta, Kentucky, opened in 2000, and it hosted a NASCAR Nationwide Series race the following year. As a 1.5-mile tri-oval, Kentucky Speedway is similar in layout to numerous other tracks on the NASCAR circuit, though its 14-degree banking is shallower than most. After being purchased by Speedway Motorsports, Inc., in 2008, efforts began to bring a NASCAR Sprint Cup Series race to the track, and two years later, an agreement was reached. The track immediately expanded seating capacity from 66,000 to more than 100,000, and starting in 2011, it has been home to the NASCAR Sprint Cup Series Quaker State 400.

Kentucky Speedway's rather shallow 14-degree banking keeps qualifying speeds lower than on some other 1.5-mile tracks. The fastest was set in 2013 at 183.636 mph, about 13 mph slower than the record for a track of that length.

Memorabilia

In 1949, Red Byron was the first champion of NASCAR's Strictly Stock Division driving the #22 Oldsmobile. Action made this eight-inch-long $\frac{1}{24}$-scale diecast model of Red's Olds in 1998.

NASCAR published its first annual Yearbook in 1950. Loaded with hundreds of photos and statistics from the 1949 season, it is one of today's most sought-after racing collectibles. It originally sold for a dollar, but can fetch more than $200 today.

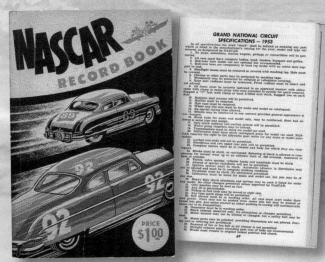

NASCAR's 1953 Record Book contained not only a history of races, winners, and points standings, but also a page of mandated car specifications. Aside from roll bars and reinforced wheels, very few changes from stock were permitted.

Glenn "Fireball" Roberts swept the 1962 Daytona Speedweeks in the Smokey Yunick-prepared #22 Pontiac. In the early 1990s, Racing Collectibles, Inc., offered collectors the chance to purchase this $\frac{1}{64}$-scale diecast model.

Memorabilia

A ticket to the first Daytona 500 at the new Daytona International Speedway allowed the purchase of a colorful program and a view of the exciting photo finish. A postcard (above) was printed to commemorate the event.

Richard Petty returned to Plymouth for the 1970 season. Jo-Han Models of Detroit released this groovy ½5-scale plastic kit of his famous #43 Superbird in 1970.

Those who used this race event brochure to order tickets to the 1970 Alabama 500 at Talladega would have seen Pete Hamilton's blue #40 Plymouth Superbird wing its way into Victory Lane.

Darrell Waltrip won back-to-back championships in the NASCAR Sprint Cup Series in 1981 and 1982 driving the #11 Mountain Dew Buick Regal. Plastic model builders rejoiced when Monogram released a 1/24-scale kit of Darrell's 1982 ride.

The ticket above granted its bearer a reserved grandstand seat at Daytona International Speedway for the 1984 Firecracker 400, in which Richard Petty nosed out Cale Yarborough to score his 200th and final victory.

Dale Earnhardt ran this specially painted Monte Carlo in the 2000 Daytona 500. The next year, Winner's Circle made a limited number of 1/64-scale diecasts packaged with a small piece of sheet metal from the actual car.

Dale Earnhardt, Jr. followed his father into the NASCAR Sprint Cup Series and Junior quickly became a fan favorite. Character Collectibles made this eight-inch-tall limited-edition figure in 2001.

CHAPTER FOUR

THE EVENTS

What began as a rag-tag group of race car drivers has since evolved into America's most popular form of motorsports. Instrumental in leading the early transition was "Big Bill" France, a tall, gangly race car driver who combined a true love for the sport with an uncanny sense of business and an unwavering long-term vision. The long road to that lofty destination has had more twists and turns than a Hollywood movie, and just as the challenges were often triggered by outside influences, the solutions sometimes came more by chance than by calculation. But the result is that NASCAR has brought racing fans nonstop action for more than 60 years, and these are among the numerous events that have contributed to the organization's phenomenal success.

Cale Yarborough and brothers Bobby and Donnie Allison engaged in a post-race "discussion" after the 1979 Daytona 500 that added a bit of drama to an already exciting race telecast.

Before NASCAR

Although auto races had been held as early as the late-1800s, stock car racing really got its start in the 1930s. One of the most prominent venues was the Daytona Beach & Road Course in Daytona Beach, Florida, a 3.2-mile oval consisting of a stretch of beach linked to an adjacent section of Highway A1A through a pair of sandy, deeply rutted turns. The track hosted numerous events in the pre-NASCAR era and brought several drivers into the limelight.

Right: *Particularly after a rain, the north turn at the famed Daytona Beach & Road Course could end up looking more like a plowed field than a section of race track.*

Right: *In dry weather, that same north turn could make a following driver feel as though he was traveling through a dust storm.*

Left and below: *Lloyd Seay was an early artisan who could make a pre-war Ford perform incredible feats.*

1947

In the early days of stock car racing, many events were held at horse racing tracks or in fields recently leveled by a road grader, and not only did they lack promotion, organization, and rules, but often, the promised prize money from gate receipts never made it into the hands of drivers. In order for the sport to flourish, some changes would have to be made, and one man took it upon himself to make them.

Right: *Everything that is NASCAR today can be traced back to the ideas and efforts of William Henry Getty France. A race car driver of considerable talent himself, "Big Bill" felt the sport of auto racing would benefit from an organized effort to promote races, fairly compensate drivers, and establish a points system to crown a champion at the end of each season. His first step toward this goal was the creation of the National Championship Stock Car Circuit in 1947.*

Right: *France's National Championship Stock Car Circuit aimed to increase benefits for drivers. Racing hero Fonty Flock stands with the handsome championship trophy he received for capturing the NCSCC title in 1947.*

Left: *In December 1947, the spic-and-span Streamline Hotel was the scene of a series of meetings that laid the groundwork for what would eventually become NASCAR. The historic hotel still stands on Highway A1A in Daytona Beach.*

1948

Below: *The very first NASCAR races were run in Modifieds, which were stripped-down street cars.*

After being formed in late 1947, NASCAR sponsored a number of races during the 1948 season, their success largely due to the promotion and planning of "Big Bill" France.

Right: *Red Byron is presented with an impressive trophy for winning a NASCAR race at the Daytona Beach & Road Course. At right is NASCAR Commissioner Erwin "Cannonball" Baker.*

Above: *Fonty Flock's #1 Ford lies in a patch of palmetto bushes after tumbling end-over-end at the Daytona Beach & Road Course. Flock was uninjured and would have better days; he's shown* **(left)** *waving to the sellout crowd as he takes the checkered flag at New Atlanta Speedway. The speedway crowd was so large that day that spectators had to stand atop the two-foot-high concrete retaining wall—without a catch fence in place.*

1949

After World War II, new cars were in short supply, production having been curtailed during the conflict. As such, they were precious commodities, and few people wanted to abuse what they could not easily replace. But the shortage was subsiding by the late 1940s, and at the second NASCAR event of the '48 season, Bill France included an experimental 10-mile "Strictly Stock Late Model" race. It proved a huge success and led to the first NASCAR Strictly Stock feature race. The die had been cast.

Below: *The crowd is on its feet as second-row starters #22 Red Byron and #19 Otis Martin cruise down the front-stretch during the pace lap of the first-ever NASCAR Strictly Stock race at Charlotte Speedway in Charlotte, North Carolina.*

Above: *A huge crowd attended the first NASCAR Strictly Stock race at Charlotte Speedway. The race featuring late-model "showroom stock" cars was an instant hit, and NASCAR President Bill France arranged more.* **Left:** *NASCAR Commissioner Erwin "Cannonball" Baker greets Red Byron after a race. Byron won the second Strictly Stock race, held at the Daytona Beach & Road Course, and went on to win the first NASCAR championship.*

1950

It would be a gradual process, but during the early 1950s, the racing of showroom-stock cars began to eclipse traditional Modifieds in popularity, and manufacturers began to take notice. Meanwhile, the opening of the first superspeedway gave a boost to NASCAR's image.

Left: *Darlington Raceway opened in 1950, the 1¼-mile paved oval becoming the first superspeedway to host a NASCAR event. The first race was called the Southern 500, and there was concern whether NASCAR Strictly Stock cars could run that fast for that long. But 50 of the 75 cars that started finished, and the race was a huge success.*

Above: *Perhaps influenced by the popularity of NASCAR's Strictly Stock Division, promoters at North Wilkesboro Speedway conducted the Wilkes County Championship Fan's Car Race.* **Right:** *Seventy-five cars filled the starting grid for the inaugural Southern 500 at Darlington Raceway.* **Far right:** *In 1950, Nash Motor Co. became the first manufacturer to actively support NASCAR racing.*

1951

The NASCAR Strictly Stock class not only attracted the attention of manufacturers but also encouraged the participation of more teams. Both were vital elements in the growth of NASCAR.

Right: The Motor City 250 at Detroit's Michigan State Fairgrounds may well be one of the most pivotal races in NASCAR history, as Bill France took NASCAR racing to the doorstep of the automotive industry. A wall-to-wall crowd of more than 16,000 watched the action-packed contest, and auto executives took notice. It wasn't long afterward that the automakers threw their support behind NASCAR.

Left: A total of 82 cars started the 1951 running of the Southern 500, proving that Strictly Stock racing was as popular with drivers as it was with spectators. It was the biggest starting field in the history of NASCAR's premier series.

1952-1954

Right: *When advance ticket sales for a NASCAR Speedway division (open-wheel) event at Darlington Raceway lagged behind expectations, a second race featuring the popular late-model stock cars was added to spur interest. A healthy crowd turned out once the late-model stocks were booked, proving their audience attraction. Dick Rathmann poses in Victory Lane with Darlington President Bob Colvin at the conclusion of the late-model stock car race.*

Left: *In one of the strangest promotional ideas for any kind of racing, Hudson team owner Ted Chester convinced driver Tim Flock to allow a pet monkey named Jocko to ride shotgun during the 1953 season. "Jocko Flocko," as the monkey became known, was a big hit with the kids but had to be let out of his contract after going berserk during a race.*

Promotional efforts were stepped up in the early 1950s as NASCAR attempted to expand its audience.

Right: *In 1954, Tim Flock drove an Oldsmobile equipped with the first two-way radio used in NASCAR's premier series. It allowed Flock to talk with his pit crew during a race, a major innovation for the day.*
Far right: *Also in 1954, NASCAR staged its first road-course event at New Jersey's Linden Airport. Both domestic and foreign cars were eligible, and the race was won by Al Keller in a Jaguar.*

1955–1957

Just as stock car racing was building momentum in the mid-1950s, fate threw a wrench into the works.

Left: *NASCAR started a Convertible Division in 1956, but it never really caught on and was disbanded in 1962. During the division's tenure, convertibles sometimes competed against hardtops in what were called Sweepstakes races, but the ragtops proved to have a distinct aerodynamic handicap on the high-speed tracks.*

Above: *With the introduction of a new overhead-valve V-8 for 1955, Chevrolet recorded its first victory in NASCAR's premier series when Fonty Flock in the #14 Chevy took the checkered flag at a race in Columbia, South Carolina.* **Right:** *Number 6 Cotton Owens boosts Pontiac's new-found performance image by giving the marque its first win in NASCAR's premier series in a 1957 race at Daytona Beach.*

In 1957, the Automobile Manufacturers Association recommended that the auto industry divorce itself from all forms of racing. This came as a serious blow to NASCAR, as most of the big teams enjoyed factory support. These teams were disbanded, and all the machinery was given to the drivers.

1958-1959

Right: *Paul Goldsmith in the #3 Pontiac takes the checkered flag in what would be the final NASCAR race at the historic Daytona Beach & Road Course in 1958.*
Far right: *Replacing the Daytona Beach & Road Course on the NASCAR schedule was the new Daytona International Speedway, a 2.5-mile tri-oval that quickly took over as the top venue on the NASCAR circuit.*
Bottom left: *The starting field is given the green flag at the start of the inaugural Daytona 500 in 1959.* **Bottom right:** *The first Daytona 500 ended in a photo finish between Johnny Beauchamp in the #73 Ford Thunderbird and Lee Petty in the #42 Oldsmobile (the #48 Chevy of Joe Weatherly was two laps down). It took NASCAR officials 61 hours to review film footage and photographic images before declaring Petty the winner.*

Out with the old, in with the new: The Daytona Beach & Road Course, considered the premier track on the NASCAR circuit, gave way to the monstrous new Daytona International Speedway—the first of what would become a series of new "tri-oval" tracks—as the '50s drew to a close.

1960-1964

The 1960s opened with the flowering of a future NASCAR legend and no small amount of turmoil. It also saw the opening of a pair of new tri-oval superspeedways in Atlanta and Charlotte, followed by a ½-mile paved track in Bristol, Tennessee.

Right: *Future star Richard Petty won his first race in NASCAR's premier series in February 1960 at Charlotte's Fairgrounds Speedway. His #43 Plymouth is shown at the inside of the fourth row.* **Far right:** *Two days before the start of the 1963 Daytona 500, famed driver Marvin Panch was involved in a crash while testing a Maserati sports car. The car overturned, pinning Panch inside. Little-known fellow driver Tiny Lund—who was in no way "tiny"—helped free Panch from the car. Unable to recover in time for the Daytona 500, Panch asked that Lund replace him as driver of the #21 Ford* **(bottom left).** *Lund responded with a Cinderella victory in the race, his first win in NASCAR's premier series.* **Bottom right:** *Two movie cameras were mounted on Larry Frank's Ford during the 1964 National 400 at Charlotte Motor Speedway to gather close-action racing footage for the film* Red Line 7000.

Due to the growing interest in NASCAR, CBS broadcast live coverage of three short preliminary races during the 1960 Daytona Speedweeks. Though the four-hour Daytona 500 wasn't shown, this represented a big step up from press coverage that was usually confined to brief newspaper articles or local radio broadcasts. The following year, ABC's *Wide World of Sports* televised several superspeedway events in a tape-delay format, and the network also ran edited half-hour race highlights.

1965–1968

In many ways, the 1965-68 time frame was among the most colorful and turbulent periods in NASCAR history. Factories had officially discontinued support after the AMA ban in 1957, but it was no real secret that all supplied "under the table" assistance to top teams. Ford went on record in '62 that it was back in the game, and Dodge and Plymouth followed suit. But all that changed when Chevrolet completely pulled the plug in 1963, Dodge and Plymouth backed out after '64 when their Hemi engines were disqualified, and Ford left in a huff after '65 when the Hemi was reinstated. Dodge, Plymouth, and Ford all soon rejoined the fray, but NASCAR's juggling act to maintain a competitive environment resulted in some interesting interpretations of the rules.

Right: *Famed rule-bending mechanic Smokey Yunick entered a radically shortened and narrowed Chevelle in the 1967 Daytona 500. It was the fastest qualifier for the race but dropped out with a blown engine.*

Above: *When NASCAR disallowed use of the Chrysler Hemi V-8 for 1965, Dodge and Plymouth pulled out in protest. With GM already gone, that left Ford in the catbird seat, and the make won 32 straight races. Due to the lack of competition, the Hemi was allowed to return at midseason, but only on short tracks, not superspeedways.* **Middle right:** *Dodge and Plymouth had been running midsize cars since 1962, and in 1967, Ford switched from big Galaxies to midsize Fairlanes.* **Left:** *A helicopter dries the rain-soaked track at Charlotte Motor Speedway in 1968.*

1969

Ford and Dodge waged an "aero" war in 1969 that didn't turn out to be the only battle of the season. The year also saw the opening of what would become the fastest—and perhaps most controversial—track on the NASCAR schedule.

Right: *Ford brought out the Torino Cobra for 1969, which featured a more aerodynamic sloped nose.* **Far right:** *Dodge countered later in the year with the Daytona (front two cars), a Charger with a pointy beak and a tall rear wing.*

Far left: *Opening in 1969 was the new Alabama Motor Speedway, better known as Talladega. Like the Daytona International Speedway, Talladega was a tri-oval, but at 2.66 miles with steep, 33-degree banking, it was longer and faster—so fast that concerns arose as to whether tires of the day could withstand lap speeds that were approaching 200 mph.* **Left:** *Those concerns caused many regular drivers to get together and boycott the first Talladega 500. But thanks in part to several planned caution flags being thrown to cool the tires, the race came off without incident.*

1970-1971

Left: *Dodge didn't build a Daytona in 1970, but the '69 models were still eligible and were run at many events. Here, Charlie Glotzbach is shown driving the #99 Daytona at the August 14, 1970, Yankee 400 at Michigan International Speedway. This race went down in NASCAR history as the first in which carburetor restrictor plates were mandated in order to reduce speeds.* **Below:** *President Richard Nixon (left) inspects the #43 Plymouth of Richard Petty (right) during a 1971 promotional tour at the White House.*

Above: *Plymouth followed in the footsteps of its Dodge cousin by bringing out its own winged wonder for 1970, the Superbird. This particular car, driven by Dr. Don Tarr, was equipped with a two-way radio that allowed Tarr—during caution periods—to relay some interesting commentary to the ABC sports announcers covering the event.* **Bottom left:** *With attendance sagging at most tracks, Charlotte Motor Speedway general manager Richard Howard formed a Chevrolet team in 1971 with Junior Johnson as manager and Charlie Glotzbach at the wheel. Howard thought the return of Chevrolet to the race tracks would boost attendance for his upcoming World 600, and he was right.*

Several momentous events marked the 1970 NASCAR season. Among other things, ABC provided live coverage of the last half of several races, a record 12 drivers led the points standings, and the final dirt-track race was held at State Fairgrounds Speedway in Raleigh, North Carolina, in September. Equally turbulent was 1971, when both Ford and Chrysler backed off on support of teams, causing many to dissolve. This left the sport in dire straights, but stepping up to help fill the financial gap was R.J. Reynolds, which sponsored not only a race at Talladega—the Talladega Winston 500—but also the entire premier series, renaming it the NASCAR Winston Cup Grand National Division. ABC televised an entire 100-mile race at Greenville-Pickens Speedway, but it would be one of the last of the "short" 100- to 125-mile NASCAR events.

1972

N ineteen seventy-two ushered in what is often referred to as NASCAR's "Modern Era." With factory support all but dried up, the schedule was reduced from 48 races to 31, and teams had to look to outside sponsors for funds. Eventually, this led to most races and even tracks taking on sponsor names. Also, "Big Bill" France stepped down, passing the NASCAR reins to his son, William Clifton France.

Above: *The only manufacturer to support a NASCAR team in 1972 was the rather unlikely American Motors Corporation. AMC entered the fray with a team run by Roger Penske that put famed road racer Mark Donohue behind the wheel. The team didn't score a victory in its first season but did win a race in '73.* **Right:** *An epic battle between two NASCAR greats took place at the October 1, 1972, Wilkes 400 at North Wilkesboro Speedway. Bobby Allison in the #12 Chevrolet and Richard Petty in the #43 Plymouth pounded each other near the finish, with Petty passing a smoking Allison on the final lap to take the win.*

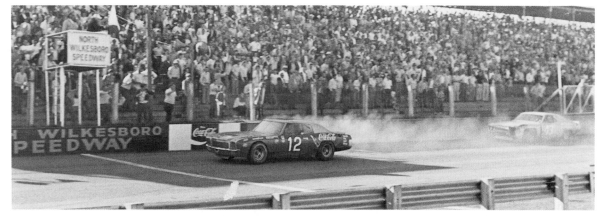

Below: *Taking over the NASCAR reins in 1972 was William Clifton France (center), son of founder "Big Bill" France. Flanking Bill France, Jr., are 1970 NASCAR champion Bobby Isaac (right) and crew chief Harry Hyde.*

1973-1974

A lack of factory support spelled the end of many teams and left others on a shoe-string budget. Then, in October 1973, the Organization of the Petroleum Exporting Countries (OPEC) announced it was cutting back on oil exports to the United States and other countries, resulting in a further setback to the sport.

Above: *In what was to be the final NASCAR victory for the Plymouth nameplate, Dick Brooks won a stunning upset in the 1973 Talladega 500 driving an unsponsored car owned by the Crawford Brothers.*

Right: *The backstretch of Talladega's Alabama International Motor Speedway is littered with wrecked cars and debris following a 21-car crash in the May 6, 1973, Winston 500. Some drivers blamed it in part on the huge 60-car starting field.* **Below:** *The length of all races was cut by 10 percent in 1974. Here, Gary Bettenhausen's #16 AMC Matador runs ahead of #83 Ramo Stott and #32 Dick Brooks in that year's Daytona 500, which lasted only 450 miles.*

In response to the late-1973 OPEC oil embargo, the government ordered that gas stations be closed between 9 P.M. Saturday and midnight on Sunday, making it harder for NASCAR fans to drive to a race. Furthermore, the government asked everyone to reduce fuel consumption by 25 percent. In response to the government's request, NASCAR shortened race lengths by 10 percent for 1974 and limited teams to 30 gallons of fuel for practice sessions. Following that year's Daytona Speedweeks activities in February, NASCAR announced it had used 30.1 percent less fuel than it had during the '73 event.

1975–1976

NASCAR gained additional television coverage in the mid-1970s, and that helped bring in more corporate sponsors.

Throughout the history of NASCAR's premier series, nearly a dozen different points systems have been used. In the early years, only the top several finishing positions earned any points at all, and different races carried different point totals based on the size of the purse. The system went through chaotic flux until 1975, when it was established that all races would carry the same number of points and drivers leading laps would get bonus points. This system was used through 2010 with only minor changes. In 2011, the points system was revised to award the winner 43 points, with a reduction of one point per finishing position. Bonus points were also awarded: three to the winner, one to any driver leading a lap, and one to the driver leading the most laps. That allowed a maximum of 48 points per race to the winner.

Above and right: *Richard Petty in the #43 Plymouth and David Pearson in the #21 Mercury had a long-running rivalry even before the 1976 Daytona 500. On the final turn of the final lap, Petty and Pearson were battling for the lead when the two cars slapped together. Both cars careened off the outside wall and into the infield grass. The engine in Petty's Plymouth stalled just 100 feet from the finish line, but Pearson managed to keep his mangled Mercury going and inched his way to the checkered flag for the victory.*

Above: *After a series of rules changes that eventually forced big-block engines to run with restrictor plates, NASCAR banned the big blocks altogether starting in 1975, when the engine-size limit was set at 358 cubic inches.*

1977-1979

After several lean years, NASCAR started to rebound in the late '70s and hit the big time thanks to a live telecast that included an exciting finish and an equally exciting post-race skirmish.

Right: *For the first time since 1949, three female drivers competed in a race at NASCAR's highest level when (left to right) Janet Guthrie, Lella Lombardi, and Christine Beckers drove in the 1977 Firecracker 400. Joining the three are three-time champion Lee Petty along with Louise Smith, who drove in the '49 race at Daytona's Beach & Road Course.*

Left: *In 1978, Cale Yarborough became the first driver to win three straight championships in NASCAR's premier series. At the following year's Daytona 500, Yarborough and Donnie Allison were battling for the win when they collided on the last lap and were both knocked out of the race. After Richard Petty blew by for the victory, Yarborough and Donnie Allison got into a post-race scuffle **(left)** that was soon joined by Donnie's brother, Bobby. Both the exciting finish and the skirmish were broadcast live by CBS Sports, and the '79 Daytona 500 has long been credited with drawing a wealth of new fans to NASCAR.*

Sunday, May 15, 1978 proved to be one of the most pivotal days in NASCAR history. Top executives at CBS announced that the network would televise the 1979 Daytona 500 live from start to finish. Never before had one of the major networks set aside four hours to televise an entire NASCAR event; previously, they usually showed only highlights. CBS anchorman Ken Squier served as an important liaison in the negotiations. "The sport of NASCAR stock car racing was coming of age," said Squier, who promoted the event as "The Great American Race." As it turned out, the race was one of the most exciting in Daytona history, with Richard Petty taking the win after leaders Donnie Allison and Cale Yarborough collided on the backstretch during the final lap. After the accident, Allison and Yarborough "discussed" the incident, which was seen on live TV. CBS easily won its time slot, netting a 10.5 Nielsen rating, along with a National Academy of Television Arts and Sciences Emmy Award for its coverage.

Broadcaster Ken Squier

1980-1982

NASCAR entered the 1980s in fine fettle, particularly considering the challenges endured during the preceding decade, and its popularity was on the rise.

Above: *After winning the Sunoco Rookie of the Year in 1979, Dale Earnhardt won the first of his seven championships in 1980. He is, so far, the only driver to have won the Sunoco Rookie of the Year and a championship in successive seasons.* **Top right:** *Bill Elliott sits in his #9 Ford awaiting the start of the CRC Chemicals Rebel 500 at Darlington in 1981. Elliott, a small-time independent driver, earned his first career pole on the tricky Darlington track in his sixth NASCAR season. He finished fourth in the race but would go on to do significantly better in later years.*

Toward the end of the 1981 season, NASCAR attracted the attention of the Entertainment Sports Programming Network (ESPN), which aired the November 8 Atlanta Journal 400 live. The network increased its NASCAR coverage throughout the 1980s, joining ABC and CBS. By decade's end, TBS had also joined in, and soon, all races were being televised.

Far left and left: *Tim Richmond's #2 Buick sits on pit road prior to the start of the 1982 World 600 at Charlotte. The car was decorated with mock sponsorship from Clyde Torkle's Chicken Pit as part of the film Stroker Ace. The comedy starred Burt Reynolds (right) as a stock car driver trying to get out of his sponsorship deal. Also appearing in the film were Loni Anderson (center) and Jim Nabors.*

1983-1984

In a repeat of the late 1960s, speeds were again on the rise, despite the smaller engines mandated since '75.

Right: *During qualifying for the 1983 Daytona 500, Cale Yarborough became the first driver to officially top the 200-mph barrier. On his second qualifying lap, Yarborough lost control and demolished his mount in a spectacular spill. Although Yarborough posted the quickest time on pole day, the car was withdrawn from the race. With that, Yarborough lost both the pole position and a notation in the record books. However, he drove a back-up car in the Daytona 500 and miraculously won the event.*

Left: *After winning the pole for a 1983 race at Charlotte Motor Speedway, Tim Richmond encountered one of the odd circumstances that sometimes arose with the many corporate sponsors active in NASCAR. Richmond won the pole for the Miller High Life 500 in an Old Milwaukee-sponsored car. He received the keys to a Ford Thunderbird passenger car after driving his Pontiac to the fastest qualifying speed.* **Bottom left:** *Richard Petty races mere inches ahead of Cale Yarborough back to the yellow flag in the final three laps of the 1984 Firecracker 400 at Daytona International Speedway. The yellow flag was thrown due to a spinout, and it was clear the race would end under caution; thus, whoever got to the flag first would win the race. It proved to be Petty's 200th and final victory.* **Left:** *President Ronald Reagan witnessed Petty's victory from the broadcast booth along with former champion Ned Jarrett, who was interviewing Reagan for Motor Racing Network. It was the first time a sitting president had attended a NASCAR race.*

1985

With big coverage and big audiences came big money, and some NASCAR drivers were on the receiving end.

Right: *NASCAR ran its first NASCAR Sprint All-Star Race in 1985. The field consisted of the previous season's race winners, which included (left to right) Cale Yarborough, Harry Gant, Darrell Waltrip, Bill Elliott, Terry Labonte, Richard Petty, Ricky Rudd, Tim Richmond, Dale Earnhardt, Benny Parsons, Geoffrey Bodine, and Bobby Allison.* **Top right:** *The day after winning the inaugural NASCAR Sprint All-Star Race, Waltrip also won the Coca-Cola 600 at Charlotte.*

Left and below: *Bill Elliott had a big year in 1985. He won the first Winston Million prize (for victories at Daytona, Talladega, and Darlington) and made the cover of* Sports Illustrated.

1986–1987

Speeds reached their peak in 1986-1987, producing qualifying times that will likely never be broken.

Below: *The 1987 NASCAR Sprint All-Star Race was an exciting event. Early in the final 10-lap dash, Geoffrey Bodine's #5 Chevrolet, Bill Elliott's #9 Ford, and Dale Earnhardt's #3 Chevrolet were running in close formation when Earnhardt forced Elliott and Bodine to spin. When the race resumed, Earnhardt led with Elliott on his tail. Earnhardt blocked Elliott's attempt to pass, and the two cars made contact. Earnhardt dropped into the infield but drove out still in the lead and went on to win.*

Of the top 30 qualifying speeds in NASCAR history, one was recorded in 1985, six in '86, and the remainder in '87. Not surprisingly, most were established at Talladega, but four were set at Daytona. Bill Elliott owns the top two positions on the list: 212.809 mph at Talladega in 1987, 212.229 at the same track in '86. He also has the fastest run at Daytona at 210.364. Other drivers in the top 10 include Bobby Allison, Davey Allison, Darrell Waltrip, Dale Earnhardt, Kyle Petty, Sterling Marlin, and Terry Labonte, all of whom have circled a track at an average of more than 210 mph.

Above: *Bill Elliott set the qualifying record at Daytona International Speedway in 1987 at 210.364 mph. Due to subsequent rules changes that limit speeds to more reasonable levels, his record will likely never be broken.* **Left:** *Ken Schrader's Ford barrel rolls down the short shute at Daytona International Speedway on the final lap of the 1987 Pepsi Firecracker 400. Schrader was battling for second place when he lost control of his car and darted into the high-speed groove. The car slid upside down across the finish line, and Schrader got credit for finishing seventh.*

1988–1989

Two of the biggest names in NASCAR racing shared wild moments at the 1988 season-opening Daytona 500, and the following year witnessed the "tire wars."

Above: *Richard Petty's spectacular crash in the 1988 Daytona 500 spewed parts all over the frontstretch. Petty brushed bumpers with Phil Barkdoll, then was hit by A. J. Foyt. Petty's #43 Pontiac tumbled for a couple hundred yards before being hit by Brett Bodine. The King was shaken up in the incident but not seriously injured.*
Right: *At the end of the Daytona 500, Bobby Allison's #12 Buick crossed the finish line two car lengths ahead of runner-up Davey Allison's #28 Ford. The 1-2 finish by father and son was the first since Lee and Richard Petty ran 1-2 at a race in 1960.*

Below: *The Indiana-based Hoosier Tire Company, which employed just 18 people, entered NASCAR racing in 1988. After Hoosier-shod cars scored more than a dozen victories, the tiny company pulled out at the end of the 1989 season, having successfully gone toe-to-toe with corporate giant Goodyear.*

133

1990-1993

The 1990s opened with a mix of highs and lows, but the popularity of NASCAR continued to grow.

Left and far left: *For the film* Days of Thunder, *NASCAR allowed the #46 Chevrolet of Greg Sacks and a few other cars to run with in-car cameras during the 1990 Daytona Speedweeks events in order to record authentic racing footage. The film starred Tom Cruise as Cole Trickle, a brash, cocky, but talented driver. Nicole Kidman co-starred as neurosurgeon Dr. Claire Lewicki. Trickle's crew chief, Harry Hogge, was played by Robert Duvall.*

Far left: *On June 7, 1992, NASCAR founder William Henry Getty "Big Bill" France passed away in Florida at the age of 82.* **Left:** *Rusty Wallace in the #2 Pontiac and Dale Earnhardt in the #3 Chevrolet honor Davey Allison and Alan Kulwicki with a Polish victory lap (run opposite of normal direction) after the 1993 Hooters 500, which Wallace won and in which Earnhardt clinched his sixth championship. Allison and Kulwicki both died during the year, Allison in a helicopter crash, Kulwicki in a plane crash.*

1994-1997

Anew race at an old track highlights the mid-1990s. NASCAR is on fire, and larger audiences along with big money fan the flames.

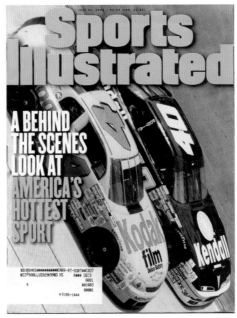

Left: *The cover story of the July 24, 1995, issue of* Sports Illustrated *put NASCAR racing on the map with traditional "stick-and-ball" sports. Interest in NASCAR was growing, and the SI article helped introduce sports fans to its unique form of racing.*

Above: *The inaugural Brickyard 400 took place in 1994 at the Indianapolis Motor Speedway, marking the first time the famed track had hosted a NASCAR event. Eventual winner Jeff Gordon is shown driving the #24 DuPont Chevrolet.*
Right: *Jeff Gordon noses out Jeff Burton to win the 1997 Mountain Dew Southern 500. With that, Gordon became only the second driver to win the Winston Million bonus.*

Trackside attendance for NASCAR races was going through the roof; the 1994 tally of nearly 4.9 million was a million more than the year before. The figure topped five million in 1995, when NASCAR developed its own website, www.nascar.com.

1998-1999

The racing was hotter and the prizes bigger as NASCAR closed out its fifth full decade of action-packed racing.

Right: *Dale Earnhardt leads a pack of cars as they approach the white flag to enter the final lap of the 1998 Daytona 500. The race ended under caution, with Earnhardt finally winning the event after 20 heartbreaking years of trying.* **Far right, top:** *Crews of virtually every team lined up to congratulate Earnhardt on his victory.* **Far right, middle:** *Jeff Gordon follows an armored car spewing million dollar bills with Gordon's likeness on them at the conclusion of the 1998 Pepsi Southern 500 at Darlington Raceway. Gordon won the No Bull 5 bonus, which replaced the Winston Million.* **Far right, bottom:** *In his first race in NASCAR's premier series, Dale Earnhardt, Jr., trails his famous father in the 1999 Coca-Cola 600 at Charlotte.*

2000-2001

Right: *Mike Helton succeeded Bill France, Jr. as NASCAR president in November 2000.*

The new millennium brings a change in leadership, coverage, and participants and witnesses the end of a NASCAR legend.

Left: *In 2001, Dodge returned to NASCAR's premier series, the first time the company had participated since the late '70s. Shown is the #40 Dodge of Sterling Marlin.*

Since the beginning of NASCAR television coverage, each track sold the TV rights for each event, resulting in the races being aired on several different networks. In late 1999, NASCAR consolidated coverage so that, starting in 2001, races would be primarily on FOX and NBC, with a few being shown on the TNT cable network.

Right and far right: *On the last lap of the 2001 Daytona 500, icon Dale Earnhardt lost his life in an accident. The NASCAR community paid its respects to the fallen driver throughout the 2001 season. All telecasts of NASCAR's premier series honored Earnhardt with a silent third lap, pre-race tributes were included at virtually all the events, flags were flown at half-mast, and pit crews would often line up to show their respect.*

2002-2003

A future legend begins to make his mark amidst the winds of change.

Left: *In the closest finish since NASCAR began using electronic timing, Ricky Craven in the #32 Pontiac nipped Kurt Busch by .002 seconds to win the Carolina Dodge Dealers 400 at Darlington Raceway. It would prove to be the last victory for the Pontiac nameplate.* **Below:** *Tony Stewart smokes up the frontstretch of Charlotte Motor Speedway after his victory in the 2003 UAW-GM Quality 500 in what is now a common practice with NASCAR's younger drivers.*

Above: *Jimmie Johnson in the #48 Chevrolet won his first race at the 2002 NAPA Auto Parts 500 at Auto Club Speedway in his 13th career start in NASCAR's premier series. He would go on to win many more.*
Right: *Brian France, son of Bill France, Jr., replaced his father as NASCAR Chairman and CEO in October 2003.*

2004-2005

NASCAR alters the points race by instituting the end-of-season Chase, while drivers add a touch of flair to the spectacle of racing.

Right: *NASCAR instituted the Chase for the NASCAR Sprint Cup in 2004. The top-10 drivers in the points standings after the first 26 races competed for the title over the final 10 races. The first Chase class consisted of (left to right) Dale Earnhardt, Jr., Jeff Gordon, Matt Kenseth, Tony Stewart, Jimmie Johnson, Elliott Sadler, Jeremy Mayfield, Kurt Busch, Ryan Newman, and Mark Martin. Busch won the championship.*

Above: *Matt Kenseth in the #17 Ford nips Kasey Kahne to win the 2004 Subway 400, the final race at the Rockingham Speedway for NASCAR's premier series.* **Far left:** *Tony Stewart and crew scale the fence at Indianapolis Motor Speedway following the team's win in the 2005 Allstate 400 at the Brickyard.* **Left:** *After winning his first race in the 2005 Golden Corral 500, Carl Edwards performed his trademark backflip off the window-sill of his car.*

2006-2007

After years of development, a new generation of race car makes a successful debut, and the NASCAR family loses a former leader.

Right: *Brett Bodine, NASCAR's director of cost research, tests a Dodge version of NASCAR's new car design before the 2006 Daytona 500. The new car was a seven-year project designed to improve safety for drivers and reduce costs for teams. NASCAR announced plans to run the new car in 16 races during 2007, 26 in '08, and full-time in '09.*
Right: *Toyota joined the NASCAR fray in 2007 with cars bearing the "Camry" name. Since both the "old" car and the new car were raced in 2007, Toyota had to build one of each design; shown is the new version.*
Right: *The NASCAR family mourned the loss of former Chairman and CEO Bill France, Jr., who died June 4, 2007, at the age of 74.*

Left: *Jimmie Johnson (left) celebrates his first championship in 2006 with team owner Rick Hendrick (center) and crew chief Chad Knaus.*
Below: *Bristol Motor Speedway hosted the first race for the new car in March 2007. The Food City 500 was won by Kyle Busch in the #5 Chevrolet.*

2008-2009

One of NASCAR's biggest stars wins a record four consecutive championships.

Right: *Dale Jarrett, 1999 NASCAR champion, ran his last event at the NASCAR Sprint All-Star Race in May 2008. He went on to become a race commentator for ESPN.* **Middle right:** *Eleven of the 12 participating drivers in Bristol Motor Speedway's "Saturday Night Special" exhibition race in March 2009 pose before the event. The race was open to past NASCAR Nationwide and NASCAR Sprint Cup winners at the speedway and was run in stock cars painted to resemble the drivers' old rides. Pictured left to right are David Green, Terry Labonte, Jack Ingram, Harry Gant, Rusty Wallace, Phil Parsons, former race queen Linda Vaughn, Larry Pearson, Cale Yarborough, L. D. Ottinger, Jimmy Spencer, and Sterling Marlin. Junior Johnson was not present for the photo. The event was so popular that it was scheduled to be run again in 2010.* **Right:** *Jimmie Johnson won his fourth straight championship in 2009, a new NASCAR record.*

Left: *Toyota's first win in NASCAR Sprint Cup Series competition came when Kyle Busch won the Kobalt Tools 500 at Atlanta Motor Speedway in March 2008. It was the first victory for a foreign car at the NASCAR Sprint Cup Series level since 1954, when Al Keller won with a Jaguar in NASCAR's first road-course race in Linden, New Jersey.* **Below:** *Jimmie Johnson does a burnout on Las Vegas Boulevard in front of the Wynn Hotel as part of the NASCAR Sprint Cup Series Victory Lap. The city of Las Vegas closed the boulevard and allowed the top-12 drivers in the points standings to cruise "The Strip" in their cars. The parade was part of Champion's Week in December 2009.*

2010-2012

NASCAR rewrites the rule book with the goal of increasing competition.

Right: *In January of 2010, NASCAR officials announced several rule changes that would go into effect that year. Many of the changes encouraged closer competition, something that was clarified when NASCAR told the drivers, "Have at it, boys."*

Right: *Brad Keselowski's #12 Dodge takes flight after being hit by Carl Edwards' Ford in the 2010 Kobalt Tools 500 at Atlanta Motor Speedway. In the era of "Have at it," the Edwards-Keselowski feud was one of the most dramatic.*

Right: *Trevor Bayne, in the Wood Brothers #21 Ford, leads #99 Carl Edwards and #34 David Gilliland across the finish line in the 2011 Daytona 500. The 20-year-old Bayne stunned the stock car world by winning the Daytona 500 in only his second NASCAR Sprint Cup Series start, and became the youngest driver to ever win the Daytona 500. It also marked Ford's 600th NASCAR Sprint Cup Series victory.*

Left: *Junior Nation had waited 143 races for this day. Dale Earnhardt, Jr., takes the checkered flag in the 2012 Quicken Loans 400 in June at Michigan International Speedway. During qualifying on the newly paved track, Marcos Ambrose put his Ford on the pole with a speed of 203.241 mph, the first 200 mph-plus qualifying lap on a track outside of Talladega and Daytona.*

Above: *In the 2012 running of the AdvoCare 500 on November 11 at Phoenix International Raceway, Jeff Gordon decided that enough was enough. After a series of run-ins with Clint Bowyer over the course of the season, Bowyer shoved Gordon into the wall toward the end of the race. Gordon waited until the last lap to get his revenge on Bowyer, who was running fifth at the time and was in contention for the championship. Gordon drove slowly along the apron of the track waiting for Bowyer to come around, and then sharply turned into Bowyer, sending him nose-first into the wall. Two days later, Gordon was fined $100,000 and 25 points for actions detrimental to stock car racing.*

2013

A new generation of car hits the track, and some established drivers – and teams – make news.

Right: *The 2013 NASCAR Sprint Cup Series season saw the introduction of the new Gen-6 race car. The new Chevrolet SS (bottom), Ford Fusion (middle), and Toyota Camry (top) bore a much closer resemblance to their street counterparts than did the Gen-5 cars.*

Left: *In the days after the September 7th Federated Auto Parts 400, NASCAR studied video and audio tapes that convinced them that Michael Waltrip Racing had intentionally manipulated the finishing order of the race and the championship race as well. NASCAR fined Michael Waltrip Racing $300,000, suspended general manager Ty Norris, and penalized each of the three teams 50 points. The point penalty bumped MWR driver Martin Truex, Jr., from the Chase for the NASCAR Sprint Cup, and moved Ryan Newman back in. Six days after the race, NASCAR allowed Jeff Gordon to join the Chase as well.*

Right: *Tony Stewart sits in his custom-made wheelchair in September after breaking his right leg in a sprint-car crash the previous month. Before the injury, he had started 521 consecutive NASCAR Sprint Cup Series races dating back to 1999. An early season win at Dover allowed him to continue a 15-year streak of winning at least one race every season – the longest active streak in the series' history.*

Left: *Jimmie Johnson hoists the NASCAR Sprint Cup Series championship trophy for the sixth time in eight years. With that, Johnson became the youngest driver to win six championships, and also won them the fastest. Only Richard Petty and Dale Earnhardt have won more championships, with seven each. Johnson started 2013 with his second Daytona 500 win, and added five more victories during the year. He led more laps during the season than any other driver, and never sat lower than third in the points standings.*

Right: *With seven laps to go in the September 7th Federated Auto Parts 400 at Richmond International Raceway, Clint Bowyer spun by himself coming off turn four. The single-car incident looked innocent enough at the time, but after the race was over, fingers began to point at a conspiracy inside the Michael Waltrip Racing team. Bowyer's spin and later green-flag pit stops by Bowyer and fellow MWR team member Brian Vickers allowed MWR teammate Martin Truex, Jr., to make the Chase for the NASCAR Sprint Cup while bumping Ryan Newman and Jeff Gordon out of contention.*

2014

The competition changes up with new points and new faces.

Right: Dale Earnhardt, Jr. celebrates after winning the rain-delayed Daytona 500. Earnhardt, Jr.'s second Daytona 500 win broke a 55-race dry spell. On lap 146 of 200, there was the first of four multicar accidents. Despite the crashes, 20 cars finished on the lead lap.

Left: On January 30, 2014, NASCAR announced a change to Chase for the NASCAR Sprint Cup Championship eligibility. The top 15 drivers with wins after the 26th race automatically transfer to the Chase grid. The 16th spot is for the points leader, if that driver does not already have a win. If there are fewer than 15 winners, the Chase grid will be filled with the winless drivers highest in points. The Chase will have four rounds. After each round, the three lowest-ranked drivers will be eliminated, leaving four drivers to compete for the NASCAR Sprint Cup Series Championship.

Right: Jimmie Johnson runs a backward victory lap after the May 25 Coca-Cola 600 at Charlotte Motor Speedway. Johnson led 164 of the 400 laps and beat Kevin Harvick by just 1.2 seconds of a four-hour race.

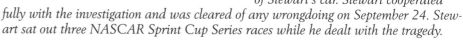

Left: On August 29, Tony Stewart spoke for the first time since a fatal sprint-car accident at Canandaigua Motorsports Park in upstate New York. On August 9, local driver Kevin Ward Jr.'s car spun and came to a stop against the outside wall, where he exited the vehicle and walked onto the track's surface to confront Stewart. As Stewart came around, Ward Jr. was struck and killed by the right rear tire of Stewart's car. Stewart cooperated fully with the investigation and was cleared of any wrongdoing on September 24. Stewart sat out three NASCAR Sprint Cup Series races while he dealt with the tragedy.

Right: In 2014, Joey Logano had his breakout year with career-best five wins, 16 top five, and 22 top 10s. He entered the final race at Homestead with a shot at the NASCAR Sprint Cup Series Championship. Logano came to pit road in sixth but the car fell off the jack and Logano fell to 21st. He only made it back to 16th before the race ended and finished fourth in the final point standings.

Right: In 2014, Kyle Busch and Denny Hamlin accounted for Toyota's two victories, down from 14 in 2013. Toyota Racing Development flagbearers Joe Gibbs Racing and Michael Waltrip Racing appeared as though they had fewer horsepower than did other manufacturers.

Left: Kevin Harvick's #4 Budweiser Racing team was strong at Daytona and won at Phoenix, Darlington, and Charlotte. Bad luck in Atlanta and Dover cost the team possible victories. Harvick, who is known as "The Closer," finished the season with a second-place finish at Texas and back-to-back wins at Phoenix and Homestead. Harvick led the most laps and miles in 2014 by large margins and won the most poles with eight. The 2014 season with five wins was his best since he won five times in 2006.